—

Why Knowing
God Is Better
Than Knowing
It All

for all who wander

B&H
PUBLISHING
NASHVILLE, TENNESSEE

(in)courage author
robin dance

Published by B&H Publishing Group
Nashville, Tennessee

Dewey Decimal Classification: 248.84
Subject Heading: BELIEF AND DOUBT / FAITH / CHRISTIAN LIFE

Unless otherwise noted, all Scripture quotations are taken
from the Christian Standard Bible®, Copyright © 2017 by Holman
Bible Publishers. Used by permission. Christian Standard Bible® and
CSB® are federally registered trademarks of Holman Bible Publishers.

Also used: English Standard Version (ESV), Text Edition: 2016.
Copyright © 2001 by Crossway Bibles, a publishing ministry
of Good News Publishers.

Also used: New International Version (NIV), copyright ©1973, 1978, 1984,
2011 by Biblica, Inc.® Used by permission. All rights reserved worldwide.

Also used: New American Standard Bible (NASB),
copyright © 1960, 1962, 1963, 1968, 1971, 1972, 1973,
1975, 1977, 1995 by The Lockman Foundation.

Cover design by Faceout Studio; Lindy Martin. Cover images: CACTUS
Creative Studio/stocksy; jumpingsack/shutterstock; ilolab/shutterstock; Art
Stocker/shutterstock; arigato/shutterstock. Author photo © Jennifer Faris.

1 2 3 4 5 6 7 • 24 23 22 21 20

To Lora,
My first best friend, my biggest cheerleader,
and the big sister God knew I would need in this life,

and

To my father-in-love, Tommy, for faithfully showing me
what it looks like to live out Matthew 6:33.

ACKNOWLEDGMENTS

A lovely surprise I discovered about writing a book is it honest-to-goodness takes a village. I had some misguided notion it was all about the author and her longhand or laptop, but I've learned many, many people contribute to what readers ultimately hold in their hands. They are the unheralded secret sauce for authors, and without them, we're doomed. So, it is with great affection and in all sincerity, I offer my deepest gratitude:

To Steven Pressfield. I am certain it was God Himself who placed your book in my hands precisely when I needed it—just before I was given opportunity to write my book. *The War of Art* was at first a crutch, and then a kick in the behind every time I needed one.

To Jen, who first introduced me to blogging by sharing her own beautiful words.

To longtime PENSIEVE readers, to those who've followed my words when I transitioned my blog, and to brand-new friends, thank you for ever reading my words and offering your encouragement. I do not take it for granted, and I'm honored and humbled that you would give me a second of your time.

To Stephanie Bryant and Holley Gerth. Who would've imagined that my tentative "yes" to write for some new website you were founding could one day lead to this? You've quietly continued to inspire and encourage me, and one day I might just have to *blawg you.*

To DaySpring, LifeWay, and B&H Publishing. Saul Robles and Janie McReynolds, there was no way you could have known how incredible the timing of your invitation was to write this book; even a year earlier would have been too soon. Saul, thank you for your steadfast support and leadership for all these years and for believing in me now. Janie, I'm so glad *you* were the one tasked with bringing me on board. Your early enthusiasm set a beautiful stage. Devin Maddox, your ability to hear my heart as a writer astounded me, and I'm grateful beyond words for the freedom you extended to me—a relatively unknown first-time author—to write a memoir. It is a gift I do not take for granted.

To Mary Carver. We've been in it for the long haul, haven't we? Your insight and work on the prescriptive pieces for the Journey Guide are invaluable. Plus, you always seemed to have just the right words I needed to hear when I was all wobbly.

To Joy Groblebe. God must be especially fond of me to have allowed me the privilege of working with and learning from you. You're an absolute rock star for knowing when I needed you to crack a whip or hold my hand. This book is better because of you.

To Ashley Gorman. Working with you has been an absolute delight, and I cannot imagine my words in any more capable hands than yours. Truly, I am spoiled going forward because you do your job so well. Thank you for how you thoroughly answered every question, for giving shape and direction to my story for reader benefit, and for tenderly offering me grace when I needed it. I am your biggest fan.

To Mary Wiley and Jenaye White, a dynamic duo if ever there was one! There's so much you bring to the book marketing and PR table, wisdom and insight beyond your years. Your enthusiasm, encouragement, confidence, and kindness made you perfect coaches for me, and I'm beyond grateful for your support and hard work.

To my co-(in)courage contributors. For ten years you have inspired me by pointing me to Jesus through your beautiful words and stories. You have influenced me in the best of ways, and I'm thankful our lives are intertwined now and forever.

To our (in)courage reading community. You are incredible women of courage and grace, and you have blessed me in ways large and small. Our first ten years together have been special, haven't they? How 'bout ten more?

ACKNOWLEDGMENTS

To my prayer team. That you said "yes" when I asked for help, consistently prayed for me during the second half of my book, were willing to pray daily at a specific time, and emailed encouragement when I needed it most, I am humbled but thankful. I felt your prayers.

To hope*writers Authors Connect. Oh my . . . the timing of our little circle came at just the right time. Thank you for your wise counsel, enthusiastic encouragement, insight and observations, and friendship.

To Tsh Oxenreider. Our late-night retreat talks were some of my favorites, and I'm grateful our online lives crossed into real life. Thank you, too, for seeing me at a time I needed to be seen, and for the honor of writing for Simple Mom and then The Art of Simple.

To Patsy Clairmont and Liz Higgs. On more than one occasion you have extended a rare sort of generosity toward me that has meant more than you can possibly know. You have given without any expectation of receiving in return, teaching me much in the process. I admire and appreciate you both on a thousand different levels.

To Grace Writers. Kris and Elizabeth, our little circle of three may be small but it's mighty. Then, again, didn't a wise man once say, "A cord of three strands is not easily broken"? Thank you for listening well, praying hard, and offering your hearts in friendship.

To Shelly Wildman and Richella Parham. The "Class of '63" is special, isn't she? I am indebted to you for your wisdom, encouragement, and honest counsel. You aren't just two of the best *writers* I know, you're two of the best *humans*. Your friendship is a dear and precious thing.

To my Best Girls. Bonnie, Diane, Mary, and Susan . . . who knew Voxer could cement a friendship? The four of you have been beautiful Gap Standers in my life, women who dared to pray boldly when I put limits on God. Your encouragement has been fuel to my faith and spurred confidence in writing this book. I love you and thank God for you.

To my First Pres and CBS sisters. I have found the most beautiful sense of community among you. What a joy to see so many women seeking truth through the study of God's Word, and then pouring out what you have learned so we all can know God better. I've felt like a broken record asking you to pray for me as I wrote this book, and yet you always prayed. You are difference makers. Saynor, Gina, and Joan, your leadership is a blessing.

To Macon-Bibb Word Weavers. How much do I love *your* influence showing up in the pages of this book? Your gentle critiques strengthened my writing. And, Jeannie and Dena, "that day" your encouragement was just what I needed to keep going.

To Pastor John. You blessed me as a pastor through your careful handling of God's Word, and then again as a sounding board as I worked through some tough parts of this book. I appreciate your honesty, insight, and encouragement (and also your loyalty to a church you dearly love). I thank God often for the lifeline He threw me through one of your sermons when I didn't know what to do with my doubt.

To Tracey. How do I love thee? Let me count the ways—gold trinket dishes and vintage ashtrays. Precipice. Tears and cheers over my writing. How you laughed *at me* when you noticed my "ankle monitor." Your handmade cards. Your hand-crafted jewelry. Introducing me to Moira Rose. Your style sense. My life is exponentially better with you in it.

To Rich and Theresa. Who knew that texting daily gifs could be a ministry of encouragement? I'm pretty sure you set a world record for most consecutive days. And how did I get so lucky to have a friend-turned-publicist? Your enthusiasm and support has been a frequent shot of vitamin D, but your lifetime friendship is priceless treasure. #AgapeForever

To Joe and Dawn. Your esteem of the Lord and love of Scripture has always inspired me, and I'm thankful for the all-too-brief season we walked together. Thank you, too, for helping me fill in some blanks when I had questions.

To Cassie D, a bad mama jama, my little oven, and favorite roomie. I never get enough of you, and I only have to think of you to hear your voice in my head (*Now, Robin . . .*). I will forever be grateful to God (and Kappa Alpha Theta) for giving you to me as my second sister. I love you!

To my Gifties. Courtney, Hannah, Leigh, and Monica, you are iron-sisters, a little but mighty legion, sharpening my faith and always, *always*, pointing me to Jesus. The ways you love me, the way you are *for* me, the many times you have prayed on my behalf, lifted my arms, and believed in me has healed broken places. You have changed my life, individually and collectively, and I couldn't love you more if I tried.

To Tommy and Sarah. You have loved fully and well, impacting generations. I am favored to be your daughter-in-love. And, in the hardest trial of your life, you're still pointing to Jesus. Well done, good and faithful servants. I love you dearly.

To Jody C. Your questions early on were so insightful, and I'm grateful for how you helped me think through what it would take to write a book. I needed a deep thinker like you, and your encouragement meant more than you know.

To Lora. I cannot imagine a better cheerleader, nor can I imagine my world without you in it. Your superpower is generosity, and you're a miracle working, unsung hero in my book. Don't tell the others, but you're also my favorite sister.

To Rachel, Thomas, and Stephen. You have challenged, changed, and inspired me in the best of ways, and being your mother is my greatest privilege and joy in this life (3 John 4). I couldn't be more proud of you if I tried, and I love you with every inch of my heart.

To Tad. It is hard to even remember my life before knowing you, and I'm beyond thankful for the ways you *still* love me all these years later. To know we're in this life *together* makes it so much better; I'm excited for all of our days to come! And though you've heard it often, it bears repeating: I love you more today than yesterday, but not as much as tomorrow.

To Jesus. Thank You for Your faithfulness, for opening my eyes to see what was always there, and for loving me no matter what. I am certain that writing this book was a perfectly-timed invitation from You and gift for me, and my greatest hope is to have served You well. The better I know You, the more I love You.

CONTENTS

INTRODUCTION

Long before I poured myself into writing this book, I lived it. What I'll share with you in the pages to come, the hard parts anyway, wasn't something I could talk about at the time (a lie I bought into hook, line, and sinker, incidentally). For a gal who's been in the church as long as she can remember, that would've been blasphemy.

For years I wandered in a spiritual desert, questioning God, seesawing between belief and doubt, and generally struggling in my faith. There were things I had long professed to believe, and yet, I realized that maybe I no longer believed them. Had I ever?

The oddest part, or maybe the saddest part, is you wouldn't have known I was wrestling with my faith, and even at times, wondering what it would be like to leave Christianity or formal religion behind. When you saw me at church every Sunday, you couldn't have imagined the inner dialogue. I still believed the Judeo-Christian ethic provided a positive framework for raising my children compared to other alternatives. I recognized the benefit of instilling biblical values. And there was my life-long residency in the Bible Belt—a land where most folks presume you're a Christian. I wasn't about to disrupt the lives of my children. But secretly, on the inside, I was genuinely struggling and I hated myself for not being able to *just believe.*

I've spent the better part of a year lassoing memories and herding them into some sort of logical order for you, which makes what I'm about to say next sound counterintuitive: I hope this isn't the book you need to read.

That's the mama in me speaking, of course, the part of me that wants to protect you from any sort of pain and spare you from learning the hard way. But that's not realistic, and it's certainly not the way of

1

Jesus. The testing of our faith is a "when not if" reality for the believer, and it is accomplishing holy work. Shame on me for wanting to interfere, implying I know better than God. I shudder at my audacity.

I do envy the believer whose faith comes with uncomplicated acceptance, who doesn't struggle with doubt or become mired in endless questions. When I was younger, I was a "God said it. I believe it. That settles it." sort of Christian. Yet, somewhere along the way, things were no longer that simple.

> The testing of our faith is a "when not if" reality for the believer, and it is accomplishing holy work.

If you find yourself "needing" to read this book, that means you (or someone close to you) might be facing your own season of wandering. You're nodding as you read, understanding what I mean from the inside out. Should you find your story within the pages of mine, you'll find the relief that comes from discovering you are not the only one with a tilted or tarnished halo as you struggle with hard questions. But here's the thing I'm learning: I'd rather have a crooked halo and a refined faith than the other way around.

As I began talking with family, friends, and colleagues about this book and its subject matter—struggling with value and purpose in addition to years of spiritual wandering—I was surprised to hear a recurring theme: "I've gone through the same thing. My circumstances were different, but I know exactly what you're talking about . . ." Eventually they'd go on to explain their version of my story. Hearing account after account of struggle, I realized though all of us are unique, the Ecclesiastical writer was right: "there is nothing new under the sun" (Eccles. 1:9b). Though each of us has a one-of-a-kind DNA and the details of our wrestling differ in many ways, we all face difficult times of testing. We also bear the consequences of poor or misguided decisions.

As I listened to each story, I began to suspect we *all* eventually wander our way through rough and dark moments. Except when it had been me, I felt like I was the only one. I assumed I was alone in my mascarade—looking like I had it all figured out on the outside, but on the inside knowing there was this scraggly little ragamuffin, quietly struggling in her faith and calling. I don't know how many Sundays I sat in church and rewrote the lyrics to songs in my head, because to sing them as they were written would be a lie.

I was doing everything I had always done, attending church and Sunday school and a mid-week Bible study. I listened to Christian music and served others. After countless years of living out my faith, I can't say when I began going through the motions. I failed to notice when practicing my faith had given way to performance.

My heart subtly shifted and doubts began to demand more attention than Truth. When exactly did I slip off the narrow path to wander toward the desert? The step was imperceptible. I don't even know if I realized how empty I was, but looking back, it is obvious how desperate I was to fill the void that my faith in God once filled. Again, I found myself in Solomon's words in Ecclesiastes—

> When I considered all that I had accomplished and what
> I had labored to achieve, I found everything to be futile
> and a pursuit of the wind. There was nothing to be gained
> under the sun. (Eccles. 2:11)

The problem with those who chase after the wind is they usually get exactly what they've been pursuing—a lot of air. And that's what happened to me. In so many ways, I was my own worst enemy.

There is something crucial to keep in mind, regardless of the strength of your faith and the surety of living out your Kingdom calling: there is another enemy lurking outside of you, and he does not want your wandering to lead to God. He is ferocious and unrelenting and he knows how to attack with precision, steering you off course. He's cunning and subtle and a master of disguise, and our misery and misfortune is his delight. He knows he's lost the war over your soul, but in his few breaths left on this earth, he spends his time trying to make you lose the daily battles of faith. Why do we let him win *any* battles when the war is already won?

Given the enemies within and without, one thing is for sure: there are no easy answers, quick-fixes, or painless tactics when your long-held but untested faith is being deconstructed and rebuilt. Be gentle, Christian, to yourself or anyone in your life who may be asking questions. God isn't offended—in fact, He is the one in this equation who is *not* the enemy—so there is no need for you to be defensive. Asking questions or expressing doubt doesn't necessarily mean you (or a person you love) are running from God; it might mean you (or she) are inching closer to Him. Give yourself, or the people in your life who are struggling, the grace and space to return. And remember: You aren't the only one praying for yourself (or them). Jesus is interceding as well (Heb. 7:25). Jesus Himself is praying for *you*!

> Asking questions or expressing doubt doesn't necessarily mean you are running from God; it might mean you are inching closer to Him.

This we know: for those who follow Jesus, faith is an anchor, a compass, our hope; when life's storms arrive at the door, faith is the steady foundation that moors, secures, and reassures us.

But what happens when that faith you were so sure about not so long ago, is no longer quite as certain? What do you do when Sunday school answers aren't enough? What do you do when life isn't turning out as you imagined and you're bewildered by how you got "here"? You know that Scripture tells you that God has a purpose for your life and yet you feel lost, or purposeless, or both. You believe salvation isn't something you can lose, but your hopelessness and the convincing snarl of the enemy is leading you to wonder if you were ever really saved at all.

Take heart, friend. God still loves you just as you are, and your questions and doubts may be the very thing He's allowing in your life to woo you back to Him. He's happy for you to weed out all the cultural baggage attached to your belief system. The ideas and principles others hold as dear and true and almost on par with Scripture, may not be *your* convictions. Hear me on this: I'm not suggesting to toss out Truth as revealed in Scripture, but it's fine and good for you to let go of the things others believe that you do not—venerable traditions for tradition's sake, or maybe the sort of things that divide churches, justify injustice, or plain old gospel-contrary ideas.

If you find yourself walking in a spiritual valley right now, know that you are not alone. My wandering lasted *years*. If you're wrestling in your faith or raising a fist at God, you're in good company. I'm discovering there are many of us.

I'm probably going to break a rule by telling you from the outset how this book ends: with hope. You need to hear that even if you're skeptical and don't believe it right now. There were moments in my long wander where I demanded things of God (all praise to Him for putting up with my bratty ultimatums), and sometimes He actually gave me exactly what I begged for.

Some of you are demanding things of God right now; you're begging Him for a sign. That you've picked up this book and read this far is His gift to you, a touch from His hand, a lifeline. He is with you in this, interceding for you and patiently awaiting your return to Him. There is value in your struggle,

You are never without hope because of who Jesus is—the God who is *with* you and *for* you and *able to lead you through this.*

friend, and I'm convinced you will emerge from your wandering with a strengthened and authentic faith rooted in God's love and faithfulness, poised to live out His Kingdom purposes for you.

You are never without hope because of who Jesus is—the God who is *with* you and *for* you and *able to lead you through this.*

While we're breaking rules, I'll also let you know how this book won't end: neatly tied with a perfect bow. We won't figure out all the answers. You may still be in the middle of your own Wander Years. But I believe with all my heart you're headed in the right direction—toward a King who loves you without condition—and I'm praying you feel a little less lost and a little more found in Him. Yes, you've been disappointed in people and by circumstances, but time will reveal the redemptive value of these wounds. Redemption and light will always find us on the dark, wandering path because God is light; He never leaves nor forsakes us, and *His* faithfulness doesn't depend on *our* faithfulness.

> Redemption and light will always find us on the dark, wandering path because God is light; He never leaves nor forsakes us, and *His* faithfulness doesn't depend on *our* faithfulness.

If you need permission to admit your doubts and struggles as a believer, done. Sometimes you just need the freedom to wrestle with holy and hard things, and for someone who understands to lift your chin, look beyond your eyes and into your heart, assuring you that your questions and doubts aren't too much for God. He loves you, He is for you, He forgives you, and He wants the best for you. He can handle this. He's got you. And He wants you to know Him more intimately through the process.

Spiritual deserts can seem unending. The wandering path feels twisted and ominous. But know this: where you stand today isn't where you'll be forever. You're one step closer to where you're going and where you'll always be. And, that, my friends, is good news.

THE WAY IN A MANGER

Let's start at the very beginning
A very good place to start.[1]
—"Do-Re-Mi," *The Sound of Music*

The setting for my earliest childhood memory is in church. Although this isn't a given when you're born in the Bible Belt, it isn't a huge surprise either.

I was cast as Mary in the Beech Haven Baptist Church Yule pageant, "Putting Christ in Christmas." While I'm sure my mother's heart was bursting with pride—her baby was cast as the mother of Jesus, after all—it wasn't that impressive to me.

In fact, I was more annoyed than anything else. Joseph kept picking hay from the roof of the crèche and flicking it at me, and he had a gross habit of picking his nose, which thankfully, he didn't flick. Also, I was tangled in a sheet repurposed as some sort of Old Testament garment, and my head was wrapped in a scarf. When you're not yet four, ill-fitting costumes are a legitimate incentive to whine.

If I'm totally honest, it's hard to say whether or not I'd remember all of this apart from the two yellowed and tattered newspaper clippings I still have stuffed away in a box of treasures. Yes, our local newspaper covered the story, and hand to heart, one of the clippings captures Joseph with his finger in his nose.

We didn't stay at that church long, though I'll never know the full why behind our departure. Less than two years after the Christmas pageant, Mama would be diagnosed with terminal breast cancer. My father attended church with us only occasionally, and Mama knew she wanted a community that would surround her babies with tenderness and love when she was gone. I suspect she thought a smaller congregation would be a better fit.

First Christian became a new church home to us. It was the stuff I imagine a lot of traditional churches were made of back in the day, no matter the denomination. We sang hymns from a hymnal and every week, the Doxology. We recited the Lord's Prayer (debts, not trespasses). You could bank on a twenty-two-minute sermon. We were baptized by immersion and sang in the youth choir (when we had one); no one seemed to care that I couldn't carry a tune in a bucket. Every member sat in the same place week in and week out, so you noticed if people were absent, and you wondered why. The next time you saw them, you'd bother to ask.

Church was as comfortable and predictable as it could get. I say that as a good thing, even if the arrogant fool in me might turn my nose up at that sometimes.

Though I was too young to notice then, I imagine people felt sorry for us. Everyone would have known our heart-wrenching story. During Mama's illness, my parents divorced. She would lose her life to cancer when I was nine, and if that didn't bring enough sorrow, the loss of our beloved grandmother—with whom we spent a fair amount of time, especially during mama's many surgeries—would come cruelly and unexpectedly a year later.

For years we were wildlings in that church, my sister and brother and I, free to roam and wander wherever we chose without having a parent there to tether us. Daddy dutifully dropped us off for Sunday school and picked us up after the service, but in between we could come and go as we pleased. Mostly, it pleased us to do what we were there for. It helped that we had the sweetest, most loving and beautiful Sunday school teacher in the world, Miss Ginn, and following her, Mrs. Allgood; she knew exactly how to reel in restless tweens. What she may have lacked in Miss Ginn's youthful sweetness, she more than made up for in piety. There was never any doubt she had our best interests at heart, though her methods were dry in comparison. It's because of her I know the books of the Bible in order and can still recite the 23rd Psalm—King James version, of course. It would be a while before I knew alternate translations even existed.

I took for granted that First Christian was naturally a multi-generational church, something today's church might implement as a "strategy." To have adults of all ages interested in our well-being—men and women who invested in our spiritual formation by their instruction and example—impacted me in a way then that still lingers now.

There's a sweetness attached to the faith of my youth. It would eventually come to feel so complicated in adulthood, but back then it was simple, so easy to accept. Jesus was the Way and the Truth and the Life, and I received and I believed and that was that. "Let the little children come," Jesus told His disciples, indignant when they tried to stop them—

> People were bringing little children to him in order that he might touch them, but the disciples rebuked them. When Jesus saw it, he was indignant and said to them, "Let the little children come to me. Don't stop them, because the kingdom of God belongs to such as these. Truly, I tell you, whoever does not receive the kingdom of God like a little child will never enter it." After taking them in his arms, he laid his hands on them and blessed them. (Mark 10:13–16)

Children are malleable and trusting, spongy little learners, celebrators of the everyday miracle. All the world they see through a lens of wonder. I wish life didn't squash that out of us. "Whoever does not receive the kingdom of God like a little child will never enter it," Jesus tells His disciples, and I can't help but wonder what they thought.

Let the children come, indeed.

Mama chose First Christian Church because she sensed a Jesus-loving community who would welcome her entire family, support her through illness, and carry us through the bloody aftermath of her death. Instinctively, she understood it takes a village to raise a child, and she connected our family to a body of believers to stand in the gap for us. She pressed Daddy until he promised her he'd continue taking us to church, and he did, faithfully. In doing so, he relinquished his country club membership and sacrificed Sunday golf, his usual weekend practice before our lives changed forever.

Every Sunday he'd stack our offering on the marble top chest by the door four quarters deep, and we'd scoop it up to divide between Sunday school giving and when they passed the plate in service. The irony of my Jewish father being as consistent a giver as any good Christian is not lost on me, and it tells me God's ways are purposefully mysterious and sometimes even amusing.

I have no memories of Mama discussing her wishes for us as they related to church attendance following her death, but I'm sure of it the way you're able to read your family's story between the lines. There are the conversations you have out loud, and then there are the ones your actions speak. Both are so valuable.

First Christian Church was the first faith community I was a part of, my home church until I got married and moved away. I was a member there longer than any church I've attended since, and likely ever will be. It was the place I first professed Jesus as my Savior, where I was baptized as a child, and where I was bandaged and balmed after my mother passed away.

Before First Christian, I can't help but hold dear my first memory of church—my first memory at all—at Beech Haven Baptist. There, I met

Jesus on His birthday, sharing center stage with Emmanuel, God with us, as my mother surely treasured up all those things and pondered them in her heart (Luke 2:19).

What a gem in my Christian heritage that the Lord would orchestrate my first encounter with Jesus the same way He came into the world: in a hay-strewn manger, with (little) people all around who didn't have a clue what was actually going on.

Let the little children come.

By God's providence and my mother's purposefulness, we would subsequently be placed in the heart of a community that put into practice the words that were preached. Mama had latched onto a people who were demonstrably *for* us and carried me and my siblings when we didn't even know we needed to be held.

If you're like me, you've likely forgotten more of your life than is possible to remember. Our histories are shaping us just the same, though, aren't they? We leave each day a little different than we begin it; we undergo tiny, imperceptible changes that give shape to who we become over time. The same is true of our faith. Small changes are happening whenever we linger in God's Word, worship in song or service, celebrate the sacraments, hear sermons or hymns, or even listen to contemporary classics on the radio that stir our heart, spirit, mind, and soul. We are altered when Christ comes to us through His people—those sweet souls who are Jesus with skin on to us, who love us in word or deed. We don't always remember the turning points, but each day we spend nurturing our faith, we look a little different than the day before.

The opposite is true, too, wouldn't you think? Each day we *don't* nurture our faith, we also can look a little different than the day before. Now, I'm not about to heap guilt on or shame anyone for their spiritual disciplines or lack thereof; I'm a believer in the adage when you point one finger, there are three pointing back at you. Still, for self-examination's sake, it's good to pause and take notice of where you are spending your energy and time, and how those choices are changing you little by little.

We don't always remember the turning points, but each day we spend nurturing our faith, we look a little different than the day before.

What happens to your faith when you aren't sowing into it, when you're in seasons of apathy, malaise, doubt, questioning, unbelief, disobedience, or maybe just carelessness? These pages tell my version of this story and I already sense this question speaks to yours. Where I've landed came as a surprise. And while I'm eager to get to where we're going, we'll have to spend some time in the valley first. (Spoiler: if you're currently down in the valley or facing a mountain, you will not be in this place forever. It is accomplishing a holy work in your life, and if you don't believe that right now, friend, I'm believing for you. Hold on . . .)

In my younger years, I'd say my faith was growing—maybe not deep, but wide. It was a simple, basic, busy faith, but I was too young and immature to understand how busyness could affect my spiritual formation. As the years went by, I rarely missed church, I attended Bible studies, I served at every turn. I received the words about works in James 2 as a personal call to action.

What good is it, my brothers and sisters, if someone claims to have faith but does not have works? Can such faith save him? If a brother or sister is without clothes and lacks daily food and one of you says to them, "Go in peace, stay warm, and be well fed," but you don't give them what the body needs, what good is it? In the same way faith, if it doesn't have works, is dead by itself. But someone will say, "You have faith, and I have works." Show me your faith without works, and I will show you faith by my works. (James 2:14–18)

In all my works, though, there was something missing. Even so, I wouldn't begin to notice my confusion for a long, long while.

Though I might've argued otherwise, my *actions* suggested my faith was all about me making my way to the manger through what I could offer or accomplish. But Jesus made

> Real faith has less to do with *me* making *my way* to the manger and much more to do with *The* Way in the manger.

His way to us without our help, didn't He? Thankfully, eventually, I would come to understand that real faith has less to do with *me* making *my way* to the manger and much more to do with *The* Way in the manger.

2

LOST AT THE COUNTY FAIR

In the middle of the journey of our life I came to myself within a dark wood where the straight way was lost.[2]
—Dante Alighieri, *The Divine Comedy*

Years had passed after my debut as Mary the Mother of Jesus, when instead of basking in the light of a church stage, I found myself as a seven-year-old wandering in the lights of a county fair. Well, I suppose I should say I *lost* myself.

My nostrils sting at a memory illuminated by carnival bulbs, the scent of diesel hanging in the air. I can still hear the clack and whirr of slipshod rides, the clamor of tinny circus music. I'm an itty bitty plankton floating in an ocean of people—*why is everyone so tall?*—but none of them are my father. A split-second ago he was right in front of me, but then lights! action! and he was gone.

My heart galloped. I dammed my tears and resisted the urge to scream bloody murder. I may have known I was lost, but I sure didn't want everyone around me to know. I had a real fear that someone "bad" might get me, and I was terrified.

I scanned the crowd for a familiar face. My sister or brother would have been a welcome sight, but it was Daddy I wanted. What if I never found him? My thoughts panicked as my imagination, unbridled, raced to extremes.

Then, just like that, there he was, there they all were, casually strolling along right in front of me, eyeballing the next amusement, totally oblivious to my "disappearance" or rising hysteria.

It was the longest fifty-seven seconds of my life, and yet, they hadn't even realized I was missing.

I stuck to them like second skin after that, never letting them out of my sight. The fun potential of any ride or amusement paled in comparison to the comfort and assurance of my family.

There's a freeze-frame of this event in my mind. It's painted with incredible detail and weighted with a depth of feeling that is surprising to me, especially given how long ago it happened. That's telling, isn't it?

Being lost feels awful.

There's an important distinction about my story, however: I wasn't actually lost. I was only momentarily separated from my family. From my point of view, I was lost and afraid. But truth told another story.

> When it comes to wandering, our perception can end up getting confused with reality if we aren't careful.

The reality was though I had lost sight of my dad, he always knew where I was. I couldn't see him, but he could see me. He hadn't lost me. That thing about parents having eyes in the back of their heads? I became a believer that night.

I also learned the power of perception. It didn't matter that I wasn't actually lost, because I *thought* I was. Thinking you're lost feels just as awful as being lost.

When it comes to wandering, our perception can end up getting confused with reality if we aren't careful. What we believe about our circumstances is the only truth in that moment, unless and until we're persuaded otherwise. New information doesn't always change the reality of our situation, but it likely alters our view of reality. If we were off base, perception should shift when we receive all the facts.

That night at the fair, I believed I was lost. But had I known the truth of my circumstances—that Daddy knew exactly where I was and I was only seconds away from being reunited with my family—I wouldn't have been worried at all. There would have been no reason to be scared half to death. Instead, my misbelief informed my response (terror) and determined my course of action (frantically searching for my family).

※ ※ ※

More recently, I was driving home from a visit out of state. I had gotten a later start on my drive home than I intended, which meant darkness would fall about an hour into my trip. GPS suggested an unfamiliar route, but it was substantially quicker than alternates, and I assumed the GPS bots were trying to steer me away from bad traffic. Waze is anyone's best friend if your travel happens to take you through Spaghetti Junction (Atlanta, anyone?).

The scenery was beautiful—heavily wooded, a peaceful lake, one small town after another. As much interstate driving as I do, I appreciate roads off the truck-hammered path. Mindlessly I followed my navigator, cheerful and particularly grateful at how it introduces you to places you've never been and might have otherwise missed had you followed a traditional map and gone the same way you've driven every other time. Wondrously, the Global Positioning System constantly reroutes based on conditions, helping you avoid traffic snarls and saving you time . . .

Until it doesn't anymore.

Everything changes once you've been driving for a while, waiting on your trusty navigator to tell you where to turn (because you saw one coming up the last time you glanced at your phone), but now the little blue arrow is floating in a sea of nothingness and it suddenly dawns on you that you've wandered out of satellite range and you have no idea where you are because you weren't paying attention due to the fact that

GPS PAYS ATTENTION FOR YOU AND TELLS YOU WHEN TO TURN—and wait! the sun just set and you don't even know what town you're in and you can hear your old-school husband's voice telling your children not to rely on GPS and to look at a map before they travel so they'll have an idea of where they're going and you agree with all that but you don't necessarily practice what he preaches and now it's dark and *goodness gracious I'm scared*, but more than anything I'm FURIOUS AT MYSELF FOR RELYING ON TECHNOLOGY, FOR NOT PAYING ATTENTION, AND FOR NOT LISTENING TO THE WISDOM OF MY DARLING HUSBAND, whose voice in my head I sort of hate at the moment.

Town? I wasn't even sure what *state* I was in. If ever I was in a tight spot, this was it.

So I did what anyone would do in my predicament—I screamed at the top of my lungs and pounded my steering wheel. Remarkably, neither did much to help. I was lost in the middle of nowhere.

When my lucid self finally emerged and dialed back the crazy, I took a deep breath, pleaded with God, turned around, and headed back in the direction where I last noticed I had cell service. Fifteen minutes *that-felt-like-forever* later, I was back in business. I memorized my new route, wrote it down, and took copious screenshots of my phone lest I wandered out of range again.

Unlike when I was a child and mistakenly thought I was lost at the fair, this time I really had been lost. A big difference, however, was how long it took me to notice I had wandered off course when I was driving. When I was at the county fair, it only took a split second, but as an adult in my car, I was lost fifteen minutes before I even realized it. Even though I was actually lost this time, I didn't experience any of the terrifying companion feelings until I became clearly aware of my lostness. (Have I completely lost you yet?)

But the moment I knew I was lost? Those same feelings surfaced—fear, confusion, disorientation, frustration, anger. And the same goal loomed before me as before: to find my way back to safety. After all, the only thing you want to do when you're aware you are lost is to be found again.

Knowing you're lost is awful.

While there are some similarities between the two, what I described in my second story is essentially the opposite of my first: What I believed about my circumstances was the only truth in that moment (instead of believing I was lost, I thought I was headed in the right direction). It was the only truth until I was persuaded otherwise (instead of my father coming in view to persuade me that I wasn't actually lost when I was little, my GPS location arrow was floating in nowhere-land, revealing to me I really was). New information (no cell service) didn't change the reality of my situation but it altered my *view* of reality (I *was* lost!). If we are off base (boy howdy, was I), perception should shift when we receive all the facts (once I got the facts at the county fair, I realized I was fine, but now, I no longer had access to directions and realized I was not fine. I wasn't *actually* headed home).

"Lost and Found" may be fun when you're playing a game, but not so much when you're living it. As different as my stories are from each other—and your stories from mine—I'm guessing the associated feelings are the same. Feelings of being lost summon fear, frenzy, despair, and defeat; finding your way or realizing you aren't lost brings a sense of calm, relief, assurance, and security. That we feel so deeply when we've lost our way, whether perceived or in actuality, literally or figuratively, is telling us something important. What in the world can we learn from these stories?

Lost . . . there are so many nuances to such a small word. When we feel lost or say we're lost, it can mean a number of similar but different things. It can mean something that was not claimed or made use of, like a lost opportunity. It can mean something that we no longer possess, like a lost reputation or a lost keychain. It can mean something that is destoyed or ruined both physically or morally, like a lost soul. It can mean no longer visible, like being lost in a crowd, or being totally absorbed, like being lost in thought. It can simply mean being unable to find the way.

Ever the glass-half-full girl, I know there are good sides to lost things. That ten pounds I lost after working out six months and giving up cream and sugar in my coffee? Good riddance. A child losing his first tooth? Bring on the Tooth Fairy, silver dollars, and sweet, snaggle-toothed grins after a treasure has been found under next morning's pillow. Losing track of time because I was lost in the pages of a phenomenal book? A double win.

Though there are "lost" upsides, if you're like me, the word has more of a negative connotation. Lost keys, glasses, or remote controls every daggum day are enough to drive a sane person mad. It's tough to recover a lost reputation in the wake of poor choices. And, as terrible as it feels to be lost and aware of your predicament, there is nothing more devastating than spiritual lostness—being far from God and never having accepted His gracious gift of salvation.

> For you are saved by grace through faith, and this is not from yourselves; it is God's gift—not from works, so that no one can boast. (Eph. 2:8–9)

"Lost people," as Christians often use the term in relation to salvation, fall into one of two camps: either they've heard the gospel and rejected it, or they've never heard it at all. The first case is grievous because they're aware of what has been offered but don't care; the second group is blissfully, and unfortunately, unaware. The end result is the same—a life apart from Christ, now and throughout eternity. For the most part, in both cases, lost people don't feel bad about their lostness—either they don't know or don't care.

This is an oversimplification, for sure, but I want to make a distinction between two different types of lost people. One is spiritually lost people in a salvific sense—they aren't believers either by choice or by lack of opportunity. The other type of "lost person" is a Christian who is wrestling with doubts and questions about their faith. In this case, as opposed to the former, they'd have a hard time reconciling their honest feelings with their faith, feeling totally spiritually disoriented. They know and care about their wandering. Is it possible to be saved and yet still feel so lost?

My experience says yes. There's good news and not so good news that comes with this.

Let's start with the good news: Feeling disoriented in your faith doesn't mean you are actually lost. Much like when I couldn't see my father at the fair and thought I was lost—regardless of how it felt—he was always just a few steps ahead of me. Daddy had always known exactly where I was. My feelings in the moment didn't accurately represent reality. Likewise, once you've truly come to faith, wrestling with hard questions or struggling with doubt doesn't threaten your salvation. That you're concerned about salvation could be evidence you are saved. Why would a truly lost person even care? Your heavenly Father knows exactly where you are and He's with you every step of the way. Though at times you may feel like you've lost Him, He hasn't lost you.

God didn't leave us to wonder about the security of our salvation. Thankfully, the Holy Spirit inspired writers throughout Scripture to pen God's promises and assurances:

> Feeling disoriented in your faith doesn't mean you are actually lost.

> Though at times you may feel like you've lost God, He hasn't lost you.

But to all who did receive him, he gave them the right to become children of God, to those who believe in his name. (John 1:12)

"Then everyone who calls upon the name of the Lord will be saved." (Acts 2:21)

"My sheep hear my voice, I know them, and they follow me. I give them eternal life, and they will never perish. No one will snatch them out of my hand. My Father, who has given them to me, is greater than all. No one is able to snatch them out of the Father's hand. I and the Father are one." (John 10:27–30)

Now, the not-so-good news: a season of spiritual disorientation feels awful. Going through the motions of faith in an effort to please others or to "fake it 'til you make it" is exhausting. Questions and doubts weigh heavy, as are the guilt and shame they bring with them, particularly for those who've grown up in the church. "Could a person who's *really* saved feel this way?" you ask yourself, and you question if you were never saved in the first place because it all feels so real. Questions shape your perspective and your reality is all askew.

We're in this thing together, friend, which is so much better than wandering alone. I know the lonely way, and I don't recommend it. I'm convinced humans are not meant to live in isolation. We learn this at the genesis of Creation, smack in the middle of Eden. The enemy of our hearts has been trying to get us alone and have his way with us since the garden. It's so much easier for him to "kill, steal, and destroy" our faith and the person God calls us to be when we we're all alone in the world, or at least when we feel that way.

If you've followed Christ long enough, you've reached some high points in your faith you never want to leave, spiritual pinnacles where you've reveled in the riches of God's grace and mercy. Those are sweet seasons, where life in Christ is roses and sunshine, or milk and honey (crème brûlée for me). At your highest high your faith is on fire and Scripture is alive. You're fierce and courageous, a victor and overcomer. You're abounding in love and producing more spiritual fruit than you can give away.

And if you've followed Christ long enough, you've also trudged through a few low points from which you've longed to escape. The cruel but inevitable sort of lows that life flings at you—job loss, financial instability, broken relationships, infidelity, unmet expectations, infertility, illness, loneliness, or the death of loved ones. Beyond these universal lows common to most of us at some time or another, dreadful also is the hollow of spiritual void less easy to define. Perhaps life is going reasonably well but God seems distant or non-existent at best, and cruel at worst. You're wrestling with unbelief. Your head has answers but your heart has doubts, and you're scared to tell anyone because of what they will think and how you'll be judged. You feel guilty and ashamed.

The faith you were once so sure of doesn't make sense anymore. You've been hurt by other believers who were supposed to love you. You're disappointed in church leaders who make outrageous choices in the name of God or who bend Scripture to mean something other than what it says. You're disillusioned by the Christian celebrity culture all around you that values popularity and power over godliness. You can't reconcile pain and suffering, injustice, or even political discord in light of a good God. It would be so much easier if you could just toe the "God said it/I believe it/That settles it" party line. But you can't.

You wonder if these doubts are really just sin and disobedience. *Is my struggle a result of my past? Have I hardened my heart and lost favor with*

God? Maybe you're disconnected from community—either it doesn't exist or you don't feel safe sharing the truth of your struggle. It's too much to process alone, and there is no one there to point you back to truth.

You begin to question yourself and your calling. You've always thought God had a plan for your life and that your purpose was some sort of work for the Kingdom, but you haven't been able to figure it out yet, and you wonder if your questions and doubts have disqualified you for service.

You read your Bible. You pray. You go to church. But you see little evidence of God at work in the world . . . or in your life.

Here's the kicker: it's not that all of life is a miserable wreck (though, for some, that could be the case, I'm afraid). There are many good things going on all around you. You've lived this life of faith for a long, long while, and it's what you *want* to want, even if you don't quite buy it now. Your friends and family may not even realize what's going on in your heart and head. Because it's a largely inner battle, it is too painful and personal to speak out loud.

You feel lost. And it feels awful.

Oh, friend . . . you're forgetting who you are, and more important, you've lost sight of Whose you are.

If you're wandering in a desert, I have something to tell you. If you've made it to the other side, you already know it.

Your questions and doubts are not necessarily a sin, and they do not necessarily invalidate your salvation. In fact, they could be the very thing God is using to draw you into a deeper relationship with Him.

There is great purpose to your wander. Not a moment of it is wasted.

Just because you feel lost doesn't mean you are.

> Your questions and doubts could be the very things God is using to draw you into a deeper relationship with Him.

3

WHISKER RUBS AND PEOPLE-PLEASERS

You don't need everyone to love you,
Phin. Just a few good people.[3]
—Charity Barnum, *The Greatest Showman*

Until the spring of third grade, I thought getting lost at the fair and being separated from my family was the worst thing that could happen to you. Turns out I was wrong. Mama losing her brutal, disfiguring, five-year battle with cancer made thinking I was lost look like child's play.

Losing your mom when you're nine is like losing a limb. Your shape is forever changed. Somehow the blasted world keeps spinning and you're able to make it to another day, and then another, again and again until you arrive at today. The nearly debilitating pain you're sure will never end, one day miraculously eases just a bit, but you're still left with scars that help you remember never to forget what you lost: someone you needed, the one you loved most, and something you took for granted until it was gone. Kids are supposed to have moms.

It took me twelve years to be able to talk about my mother without crying, and even now, tears could show up uninvited at the very thought of her. Over four decades later, there are still times I feel phantom pain.

Mama's death reverberated beyond our immediate family. It didn't take long to realize others not already acquainted with our circumstances became uncomfortable when they learned our mom had died. More often than not, people assume a young child has two living parents, and when they discover otherwise they make well-meaning but stupid remarks. My little nine-year-old mind processed my observations by telling me it wasn't normal for your mother to die so young. I internalized that to mean something wasn't right about me. I wasn't normal.

One memory sticks out, the day I got my hair cut at Adam and Eve Salon. This was the day I was reborn a people-pleaser, the day I became a performer. All it took was for the hairdresser to ask me what my mom did for a living.

Within days of Mama's death I had learned how people would respond if I told them the truth (plus, it was impossible for me not to cry), so I made a split-second decision to lie. Most of the details are fuzzy—I'm guessing Mrs. Dawson, the lady who watched us while Daddy was at work, dropped me off because there was no adult standing there to help field this question. I choked back the tears that always came at the thought of Mama, an impressive feat in and of itself. I remember feeling anxious—*could she tell I was lying?*—and even guilty; *I lied to a grown-up!*

I have no idea what imaginary profession I assigned to my dead mother. As well as my nine-year-old self could steer the conversation in another direction, any direction but Mama, I did. I worried the stylist might pick up on my fib—my heart pounding so hard and fast I was sure she could see my little chest rising and falling with each beat. I couldn't wait to get out of there so I could breathe normally again.

I never told anyone what I had done, not even my big sister, my first best friend and self-designated protector. Only now am I wondering if she ever did the same thing.

My first time pretending my mom was alive would hardly be my last time, and with practice I got better at it. It wasn't difficult to justify the lie because my little charade made it easier for everyone, especially me.

Other people were able to avoid an uncomfortable, awkward conversation, and I didn't bleed out in front of strangers. Win-win.

Seems to me the odds were likely I'd become a people-pleaser, anyway. I'm a middle child. Much of what I've read about birth order suggests middle borns carry this trait. I stumbled across an interesting article that explained, in general, middle children tend to possess the following characteristics:

- People-pleasers
- Somewhat rebellious
- Thrives on friendships
- Has large social circle
- Peacemaker[4]

Check, check, check, check, check. (Although for me "somewhat rebellious" mainly shows up in my heart and spirit; not so much in any real challenge to authority.)

It's hard to tell if these traits emerged in my personality because of my God-designed genetic predisposition, my birth order, or because of my mother's death. What caused me to be shaped as a people-pleaser—nature or nurture? I suspect both contributed, though it really doesn't matter. What I do know is I wanted to please everyone around me. My father and family, teachers, friends—the butcher, the baker, the candlestick maker, and pretty much the entire universe.

I didn't want to rock the boat. I wanted to make everyone happy. I was willing to sacrifice personal preference if it meant I could accomplish those goals.

People-pleasing manifests itself a thousand different ways. If you're a pleaser, I'm sure you're already thinking what it looks like in your life. For me, this meant as a student I worked hard to get good grades and to follow class rules. At home, I was generally compliant and obedient. In friendship, I played nice and didn't make many demands. When you're a kid, people-pleasers are teacher's pets and best campers (or at least they try to be). If you're a TV Land fan or old enough to remember *Leave It to Beaver*, think more Beaver Cleaver and less Eddie Haskell; if you're aren't either, think sweet and sincere as opposed to a brown-nosing weasel.

> Golden Rule living isn't a bad thing in and of itself—unless pleasing others becomes the dominant guiding principle in your life over pleasing the Lord.

In a sense, it's Golden Rule living, which isn't a bad thing in and of itself—unless pleasing others becomes the dominant guiding principle in your life over pleasing the Lord. I wasn't good to please God—though I figured I was killing two birds with one stone. Instead, my behavior was tied to wanting people to like me. I believed if I expressed dissenting opinion, or if I tried to get my way, I'd lose favor or friendship depending on the company. It also goes back to not wanting to make you uncomfortable, because if you were uncomfortable, I was uncomfortable, and what possible good could come of that?

Father-daughter relationships can be complicated, and Daddy's and mine was no exception. Though not abusive, his manner was gruff. There was a part of me that was scared of him, and never have I wanted to strangle my sister, Lora, more than when she told him. I must've been around ten or eleven. He outright asked me if I was scared of him, and always the pleaser—and absolutely murderous toward my sister—I stammered some sort of intelligible denial. I certainly didn't want to hurt his feelings or make him mad, the stuff of a people-pleaser's nightmare.

Daddy was not one to allow us to wallow in self-pity, and through adult eyes I wonder if that was due to him not being able fully to process his own grief and emotional baggage over a lifetime. "Stop feeling sorry for yourself," was something I heard more often than I wanted to throughout my childhood. Statements like this were his way of willing his children to be strong, and though I didn't like hearing them, I think they actually helped us to be strong in the long run (or maybe a little calloused?). Even if at times I may have resented him, I loved Daddy and always wanted to please him.

Despite his sometimes brusque demeanor, I never once doubted my father's affections for me. He said "I love you" often, and bedtime prayers were always punctuated with a kiss goodnight. I adored sitting in his lap and chattering about nothing and everything. One of my favorite intimacies were his whisker rubs. The man had a dangerous five o'clock shadow and we'd beg him to rub his stubbled cheek against our baby soft faces. I don't know why we loved it so—it's like rubbing your face with sandpaper—but as soon as he stopped, we'd giggle and beg for another.

One of the most vivid memories I have of Daddy is when he, my stepmother, Patti, and my baby brother, Rick, dropped me off at college. The station wagon was emptied, my dorm room was set up, and they were about to head home. As he leaned in to hug me goodbye, he must have sensed the need to impart a little fatherly advice:

"Don't expect everyone to like you because they aren't, and you aren't going to like everybody. That's okay, that's life."

Well, alrighty . . . It wasn't what I was expecting him to say, and certainly not what I wanted to hear. But, then again, Daddy wasn't the type of person who would tell you what you wanted to hear; he'd deliver the truth as he saw it. He knew I was about to go through sorority rush, a brutal ritual if ever there was one, and he was reminding me to shore up my heart. Though we never discussed it, he understood I was a pleaser. I doubt he would even articulate "pleaser" language the way I am now, but in his own way, he was encouraging me to be me and to take rejection with a grain of salt.

To this day, those words haunt me. They're a source of inner conflict. Aren't they a sentiment contrary to life as a believer? And yet . . . *and yet* . . . it's the doggone truth. Everybody doesn't like me, and (gasp) *I don't like everybody.*

Did I really just admit that? The pleaser who's still within me is already nervous about how you'll respond, if you'll categorically dismiss anything I have to say from this point forward because you'll see me as unseating Paul as Chief Sinner.

And . . . there you go! A perfect picture of Robin the Pleaser: trying to calculate and manage the perceptions of others. It's exhausting. For most of my years I was oblivious to the role people-pleasing played in my life. When I finally recognized it, I took steps to correct it, but I well may be in recovery the rest of my days.

To avoid disappointing others and to minimize the risk of rejection, pleasers are nice. In my case, too nice, and too nice isn't honest. I acquiesced to a million little self-deceptions—taste in music, fashion, movies, books—devaluing my own opinions in deference to yours. I couldn't handle people being mad at me and often assumed fault when it wasn't mine. My self-worth was tied to how others viewed me, and praise was my currency of validation. I had a hard time admitting when my feelings were hurt, and when emotionally wounded I'd stuff down the pain until it faded. I'd avoid conflict whenever possible, but when it was inescapable, I'd become a peacekeeper and do my best to make everyone happy. Keep peace, not make peace.

In was in her Bible study, *Living Beyond Yourself,* that Beth Moore first drew a distinction between peacemakers and peacekeepers for me. Peace*keeping*, as I recall, was an effort to keep peace at all costs in relationships—peace being merely an absence of conflict—without addressing the underlying issues and therefore resulting in a false peace. Peace*making*, on the other hand, involved confronting the people or issues in opposition to one another, addressing the uncomfortable or hurtful situation, pursuing reconciliation, and creating true unity between both parties. In the face of discomfort or pain or chaos, false peace is *avoidance* while true peace is *engaging*. One runs away and the other runs toward.

This plays out every day in our relationships, friendships, marriages, or even in the workplace. Consider an example that illustrates this beautifully: I lead a small writers group in my hometown, and unintentionally I made a remark to a group member that, to her, sounded like I was calling her out about something. I had no idea she misunderstood me at the time. The next week she called to ask for clarification about why I had said what I did. I had no recollection of the exchange, and I assured her I wasn't calling her out, and that I was so thankful she let me know! A peacekeeper would have gone home and smouldered, kept her thoughts to herself, and possibly just left the group rather than confront me. Instead, this courageous woman picked up the phone, risked an uncomfortable conversation, and immediately cleared up the misunderstanding. Bravo, peacemaker!

It wouldn't surprise me to learn that the majority of people-pleasers are peacekeepers. They'll address symptoms, sure, but root problems are rarely solved. Peacekeeping is a temporary, surface treatment, which in the moment satisfies a pleaser.

So how is your walk with God affected when you're a people-pleaser or peacekeeper? Can you be these things and it not affect your faith? I don't think so. I didn't even begin to understand how I was a pleaser until well into my thirties, and it took me a long, long while after that to realize all the implications (I'm still learning). How can you fight your people-pleasing, peace-keeping inclinations when you're not even aware of what you're doing? You can't.

Without even realizing it, I handled my faith much the way I interact with people: largely based on performance. As a believer I was supposed to please God, so I "kept the peace" with Him by doing all the things "good Christians" do, saying all the things "good Christians" say, and knowing all the answers "good Christians" know. Of course, that looked different depending on my season of life. In high school, in addition to worship on Sunday, it looked like going to youth group and FCA. In college and after graduation, it was church attendance, being consistent in Bible study, having a regular quiet time, and tithing. After marriage and children, it was more of the same but I added church service and volunteering on a regular basis. Cooking meals for the bereaved, working at the Care Center, compiling a church cookbook, memorizing Scripture with my children, volunteering in the nursery, teaching Vacation Bible School, hosting in-home Bible studies. The opportunities to minister within and without church doors are endless, and I was an excellent box checker.

I looked like a model Christian, a poster child for the Proverbs 31 woman. I knew all the right things to do, to say, to believe. In one sense, I knew it all. Being a "Christian know-it-all" isn't about believing you know everything there is to know about faith; it's much more subtle than that. A Christian know-it-all loses sight of God's faithfulness and sufficiency and forgets that knowing God and making him known is paramount. You may give lip service and mental assent to those things, but the proof is in your actions. Though I would have never said it out loud, I sensed that if I didn't do and say all the right things, I would be a disappointment to God and risk His rejection. Had you asked me if I felt that way, I probably would have said no, but the truth was, I was less concerned about knowing God and growing in intimacy with Him and more concerned with knowing and doing all the things church folks expected of me. We people-pleasers

> If we're honest, sometimes a people-pleaser's biggest desire is not to know and love God. It's wanting others to think we do.

don't serve an audience of One; we're trained monkeys performing in a circus. If we're honest, sometimes our biggest desire is not to know and love God. It's wanting others to think we do.

Belief is not necessarily evidenced by what we say. Instead, belief is best evidenced by what we do—actions which always flow out of what we honestly think in the secret places of our minds and hearts. And it is a lovely thing when what you believe, say, and do perfectly align. But when they don't? You're wandering and don't even know it.

Which in the end is much rougher on a heart and soul than a whisker rub on your cheek.

4

TESTIMONY ENVY

Amazing grace! how sweet the sound,
That saved a wretch; like me!
I once was lost, but now am found,
Was blind, but now I see.[5]
—John Newton, "Amazing Grace"

Mama understood her prognosis and seized the time she had left to influence her young daughters and love our baby brother, Jason. She told Lora and me we'd win successive Miss America titles because she wanted us to feel beautiful. She let Jason drink "coffee" with her—enough milk and sugar to make it candy. She prayed with us every day. She didn't discriminate against others when everyone else seemed to do so. She told us about the birds and the bees, but the only thing I remember from *that* conversation is her shrieking, "I am NOT going to draw pictures for you!"—which I take to mean I asked too many questions. I wish we could have known each other a little while longer. I can't help but wonder how her continued influence might've helped me be less of a pleaser and navigate all those hard things a young girl must face. Like when I was twelve, and something life-changing happened to me.

I got braces.

As is common practice, in order to gauge effectiveness and quantify results, my orthodontist took "before" pictures. Bless my wide-gapped, buck-tooth heart, what a tortuous, humiliating practice for a prepubescent girl! The only thing that could have possibly added more insult to my injury would have been if they also had captured my darling face caged in full headgear.

But, oh, those glorious "after" photos of my pearly whites. Once I saw those perfectly straight teeth in a picture with that Covergirl smile, I knew it was all worth the pain, inconvenience, and indignity of a mouth full of metal.

My before-and-after pictures revealed something dramatic had happened in between the time the braces went on and came off. A powerful catalyst, the miracle-working magic of orthodontia, transformed my crooked teeth and crossbite. I was still me, but I looked like a totally new Robin.

The story of my braces, odd as it sounds, reminds me of a famous testimony in Scripture—when Saul of Tarsus was converted. I have always been a little envious of the apostle Paul's Damascus Road salvation experience. A dramatic conversion from sinner to saint lends itself to great storytelling, doesn't it? The book of Acts provides an account of Paul's incredible transformation, a spiritual rags-to-riches. Like the effect my braces had on me, coming to faith for him was painful and humbling at first, but so dramatic and transformative that he looked like a totally new Saul on the other side of it.

Let's refresh our memories on his story.

We're first introduced to a young Paul under another name, Saul, where he is basically a coat check attendant for a murderous mob in the process of stoning Stephen, a devoted Christ-follower and the church's first recorded martyr.

> They dragged him out of the city and began to stone him. And the witnesses laid their garments at the feet of a young man named Saul. (Acts 7:58)

Though Saul didn't have a direct hand in Stephen's death, he was no innocent. Acts 8:1 tells us, "Saul agreed with putting him to death." Two verses later we see a bloodthirsty Saul as he began "ravaging the church. He would enter house after house, drag off men and women, and put them in prison." By his own words he confessed, "I persecuted this Way to the death, arresting and putting both men and women in jail" (Acts 22:4), and "I actually did this in Jerusalem, and I locked up many of the saints in prison, since I had received authority for that from the chief priests. When they were put to death, I was in agreement against them" (Acts 26:10).

Saul's reputation was well known, and the disciples had good reason to fear him. Acts 26:11 reveals the lengths to which he would go to persecute the saints: "In all the synagogues I often punished them and tried to make them blaspheme. Since I was terribly enraged at them, I pursued them even to foreign cities." He was mean, relentless, and didn't play fair.

But God had different plans for Saul. For anyone with a past you're ashamed of, for everyone who believes your past is too sin-riddled to be forgiven, don't let what happened on the Damascus Road escape you.

Armed with a letter of authority from the high priest to gather up Jesus' disciples and haul them back to a Jerusalem jail, Saul set off for Damascus breathing threats and murder (Acts 9:1–2). But then God intervened in spectacular fashion, in a way no one expected: a brilliant flash of light that absolutely leveled Saul. God lasers his attention on Saul, asking him in a fascinating encounter why he's persecuting Him. And while Saul hears the voice of God, he doesn't yet recognize with whom he's speaking. So he asks.

"I am Jesus, the one you are persecuting . . . but get up and go into the city, and you will be told what you must do" (Acts 9:5b–6).

Saul's travel companions are speechless, having heard God speak but not able to understand. Saul is subsequently blinded and has to be led by hand the rest of the way. For three days he couldn't see. For three days he didn't eat or drink a thing. God instructs a man named Ananias to go to Saul and minister to him. Understandably, Ananias is reluctant because he's heard of Saul and he is suspicious of why he's there—this is the man who was persecuting Christians, after all! God puts Ananias's mind at ease by explaining He's chosen Saul to proclaim his name to the Gentiles, their kings, and to the people of Israel. Lest there be any question in anyone's minds about Ananias's role, God also gives Saul a vision of Ananias coming to lay hands on him in order to restore his sight.

When Ananias reaches Saul, he prays for his sight to be restored and for him to be filled with the Holy Spirit. Immediately something like scales fall from Saul's eyes and he can see (Acts 9:18). From that point forward, he proclaims Jesus as the Son of God. Eventually Saul would give up his Hebrew name and begin using his Roman name, Paul, likely to identify with the Gentiles to whom he was preaching, but it's also an outward indicator of his inner change. He would go on to write most of the New Testament.

What a testimony—can you imagine Paul telling you about it himself? It's so easy to anchor the incredible stories of Scripture to pages in our Bibles, forgetting, or at least losing sight, that historical accounts like this one happened to real people. The next time you hear someone share their testimony, imagine Paul describing the light, God's voice, what it felt like to be stricken blind. How would he express what it felt like to be pursued by Jesus while he was actively brutalizing His followers?

Saul's conversion was nothing short of sensational. God's revelation of Himself triggered a 180-degree turn in a man dedicated to destroying the church.

Maybe you or someone you know can personally relate to the Damascus Road. Perhaps God miraculously healed you or broke some sort of addiction in your life. Maybe you were marching in one direction, came face-to-face with Jesus, and reversed course. Maybe, like Paul, you were lost with all the baggage attached to darkness, and upon the interruption of Jesus' transforming presence, you instantly broke free, stepped into Light and discovered freedom, forgiveness, and new-ness of life. When you trace your own spiritual story, is yours a compel-ling testimony like Paul's? If so, glory be to God! If not, maybe you have struggled with the same weird "testimony-envy" that has filled my own heart on occasion.

My testimony-envy always begins with thoughts of comparison (a seldom productive and often dangerous habit): *My salvation story is bor-ing laid next to Saul's. There are so many others with gripping stories about when they came to faith, but I can't remember not being a Christian. For crying out loud, the earliest memory I can point to in life was in church!*

Sundays were rarely for sleeping in, except maybe on vacation. Blessings preceded mealtime. Bedtime prayers, a nightly ritual. Our consistent church attendance wasn't based on legalism; it was simply the rhythm of our lives. Our faith practices were as natural as breathing, second nature, the way things were.

If you were raised in the church, can you relate? We never considered there might be another way people lived.

Let me stop right here and make sure you understand I'm not say-ing growing up in church is a bad thing. Being raised in a home where faith permeates the atmosphere is good, a blessing, a position of favor. I'm thankful. How we find our way to Christ is never a competition. God is the writer of each person's story, and it is at His initiative that we turn toward Him in the first place. He desires for everyone to accept the salvation He offers to us in Christ. His inclusive invitation extends to every human who's ever drawn breath and He meets them exactly where they are—whether that be a killer in ancient Rome or a church girl in the United States. Still, when I look back on my upbringing in the church, so much of it came to me by way of osmosis, and *that,* I suspect, eventually led to a lot of questions.

I know when I made a public confession of faith because, according to the dated certificate, my sister and I were baptized at First Christian Church when I was twelve. My vague recollection suggests it was more about my fear of hell and eternal damnation than it was about love for God, my sinful ways, true repentance, or my need for a Savior. Though our gentle pastor met with us to make sure we understood what we were getting into (or was it to vet our intentions?), I wanted to be a member of our church and to be able to take part in communion. Truth be told, it was less about sacrament than it was about a mid-service snack; I had been waiting a long, long while to drink grape juice from a thimble and eat those tiny fairy crackers.

This is the point where I get all squirmy when asked about my testimony. Oh, I can talk your ears slap off the sides of your head about what God is doing in my life *today,* but I can't point to that moment when I passed from death into life. I've never been comfortable claiming my baptism as the day I was born again, and I don't know my "spiritual birthday," the date others claim as the day they were saved. This has always bothered me. (And it bothers me that it bothers me.)

I didn't understand it then, but I know now that there wasn't a true heart change in that little twelve-year-old version of me. Soon enough, I would learn all the right things to say, all the Sunday school answers good Christians are "supposed" to know. I'd learn all the right things to do. *I would know exactly how to perform.*

But God isn't interested in us knowing it all or doing it all or polishing our Christian performance, is He? It's not like we could fool Him, anyway. He knows the secrets of our hearts (Ps. 44:21b), and Psalm 139 tells us God is so well acquainted with us, He knows our thoughts even before we speak them.

If you've grown up in the church, without even realizing it, you can fall into the trap of presuming to know it all when it comes to matters of faith—how to speak, how to think, what to say, how to perform, all the Christian-y things we incorporate without even realizing it. But the humbling and refreshing news is that at whatever level we behave as if we know it all, God knows the real us exponentially more so. We see this reality at play when Jesus railed against the Pharisees' pride. They may have known it all—the law, the customs, the cultural norms—but He knew the real them, and He condemned their hypocritical performance in Matthew 23:

> "You are like whitewashed tombs, which appear beautiful
> on the outside, but inside are full of the bones of the dead
> and every kind of impurity. In the same way, on the outside
> you seem righteous to people, but inside you are full of
> hypocrisy and lawlessness." (vv. 27–28)

We may not be able to fool God, but we sure can fool ourselves and, sometimes, even a few of the people around us. Thankfully, God is omniscient, and He knows us better than we know ourselves. It is His desire for us to know Him so well that we're no longer fooling anyone.

At some point in young adulthood I began to wrestle with what counts as a "real" profession of faith. According to Romans 10:9–10, "If you confess with your mouth, 'Jesus is Lord,' and believe in your heart that God raised him from the dead, you will be saved. One believes with the heart, resulting in righteousness, and one confesses with the mouth, resulting in salvation."

Isn't that exactly what I did all those years ago? Why was I continuing to wrestle with this question?

As hard as it was for those questions to plague me, I'm so glad they did. After years of the constant back and forth in my own mind, I would eventually come to fully understand what "belief" meant—to have a relationship with Jesus. I've heard it said the difference between merely knowing *about* God and actually knowing God is eighteen inches, the distance between your head and your heart. There's something to this, and we'll see what it has looked like in my life in the pages to come.

No doubt, some of you are moving your head up and down, giving me an understanding nod because you, too, grew up in church and can't recall any other way. Perhaps you, too, don't have a dramatic memory of the moment you became a Christian, and if you're honest, you've had a little testimony envy, too.

But how in the world could a Damascus Road testimony invite even a twinge of jealousy in us? On one hand, it's ridiculous—he harmed God's people on purpose! But on the other hand, desiring a story like Paul's is so human. We tend to minimize his "before" and stand awe-struck at his "after." The way God spoke to him, touched him, and then taught him, a radical before and after with no doubt about the day of his conversion. I may have looked like a new person after my braces came off, but that was only surface deep. Paul *was* a new person.

I feel a little silly admitting this about myself. Seriously? I'm envious because my testimony isn't good enough? I think that a boring testimony disqualifies me somehow? It's stunning how we find a million ways to disqualify ourselves, isn't it? If we tried to count the reasons we tell ourselves we are less than or not enough, we wouldn't be able to get to the end of them.

The struggle may not be a bland salvation story for you, but I'd be surprised if there wasn't some battle raging in your head or heart right now—failing to be a good enough parent, spouse, friend, child, employee, boss . . . believer. Maybe it is an indication of immaturity or navel gazing, but I've also come to see how the "less than" or "not enough" label is a tool our enemy uses to cultivate defeat or despair—to shift our focus from God to ourselves, circumstances, or both. The means by which we give Satan access to our heads and hearts is regrettably subtle and inexhaustible. We're often not even aware we've opened ourselves to his deceptions, and he's cunning and relentless in his pursuit of us.

Satan's lies are believable because we forget Whose we are. When that happens, we can lose sight of (or perhaps we never fully understood) our true identity.

> The "less than" or "not enough" label is a tool our enemy uses to cultivate defeat or despair—to shift our focus from God to ourselves, circumstances, or both.

I can't recall the "plan of salvation" or the "four spiritual laws" or any manner of the gospel being presented to me by a pastor or teacher when a light bulb suddenly illuminated, signaling my need for a Savior. I only remember growing up in church and doing all the Christian-y things you do when you're born in the buckle of the Bible Belt. I cannot remember ever identifying as anything other than "Christian."

Even if my intentions were sincere, at the impressionable age of twelve I didn't know what I didn't know. While my teeth may have undergone an obvious "before and after" transformation, my heart hadn't yet.

Church has been an integral, inextricable, and influential part of my life for as long as I can remember. But I suspect for a long while, my faith wasn't really mine at all. It was more me taking on a fraction of "their" faith—whether that was pastors, loved ones, or otherwise. I was professing to believe all the things I knew in my head, but didn't *really* believe in my heart. I would have argued I *did* believe, but my actions pointed to performance, as if righteousness could be earned from the outside in.

My wander years didn't begin in a shady place or on a malicious path like Paul's. I wonder if I was already a wanderer when I made that first public profession, right in the middle of good church people, the very type of folks Paul was trying to destroy almost 2,000 years earlier. On the surface, it seems like Paul and I couldn't be more different—Paul was trying to kill the church, and I was trying to serve it. But the truth is both of us were wandering.

5

A SAME KIND OF DIFFERENT

I saw something different in them . . .[6]
—Olayinka Dada, *Blossom*

From middle school to high school, and high school to college, I remained a faithful churchgoer. I would say life was more compartmentalized for me back then, but I wonder if it was for all of us coming of age in the '80s. Youth group was a mainstay, but that was on Sunday nights. While I never turned to partying exactly, every once in a while I'd cross a line. Growing up in a big college town lends itself to such a thing.

And then came college. Out of state. Away from home. A freedom I had never known. But for all my oat sowing in college, two great things came out of it: a best friend for life and the man who would eventually become my husband.

Cassie and I were pledge sisters in a sorority we initially disdained but, thankfully, later would come to appreciate and even love. We bonded over pomping a float for the First Friday parade, an annual tradition before our college's first home football game (Go Tigers! *Clemson* Tigers, lest you get any ridiculous ideas otherwise). If you don't know what pomping is, you've missed out on a beloved/dreaded Southern tradition, usually relegated to second fiddles and bench warmers; in the case of Greek Life, lowly pledges. For the unindoctrinated, a pomp is a brightly-colored, five-and-a-half-inch square of tissue paper. Into the wee hours of morning for days on end, we'd poke our fingers into the center of a square and push it through chicken wire shrouded over a wooden skeleton.

Miraculously at the eleventh hour, we'd finish the job and give birth to a giant tissuey tiger, clearly a victor over the opposing team's sad little defeated mascot. Bless whoever played us that weekend. It was always a David and Goliath match-up, but by design, the underdog was never going to win. Ever.

Though Cassie was half a head shorter than me, she had a personality, heart, and voice the size of Texas. An older sister to three brothers, she found a way to be heard among the noise. But it was her transparency that both disarmed and attracted me, telling me things I might save until I was sure a new friend could be trusted. The more she told me about *herself*, the more I wanted to reveal about *myself*. Have you heard the expression, "free people free people"? Cassie was free, which in turn, liberated me. I couldn't believe she was so open to a stranger. Then again, we were strangers for only five minutes.

Years later when I stumbled into the pages of *The Four Loves* by C. S. Lewis, I found what she and I had discovered long ago:

> Friendship arises out of mere Companionship when two or more of the companions discover that they have in common some insight or interest or even taste which the others do not share and which, till that moment, each belied to be his own unique treasure (or burden). The typical expression of opening Friendship would be something like, "What? You too? I thought I was the only one."
>
> . . . when two such persons discover one another, when, whether with immense difficulties and semi-articulate fumblings or with what would seem to us amazing and elliptical speed, they share their vision—it is then that

Friendship is born. And instantly they stand together in an immense solitude.[7]

Cassie was a good Christian girl the way I was a good Christian girl—mostly staying out of trouble before we got to college with only a fistful of indiscretions. Neither of us were big partiers in high school, but we flirted with things we shouldn't have a time or three. I can't speak for her early transgressions, but there was that time I cruised Baxter Drive with my high school boyfriend at the wheel while my best friend, Mandy, and I slurped Sloe Gin and Sprite through a straw, giggling like the schoolgirls we were; or that New Years I learned even a thimble of champagne didn't agree with me . . . *at all.*

On the other side of doing things I knew I shouldn't, I'd feel bad about what I did. Of course, I knew it wasn't something God would approve of, but I was more concerned about Daddy and Patti (my stepmother) finding out. Always the pleaser, I didn't want to disappoint them. After a slip, I'd walk the straight and narrow for a good while to make up for what I had done . . . until it was time to stretch a pinkie toe over the line again. The cycle of transgressions and penance would continue, losing favor and then earning it back over and over. Apparently, this is how people-pleasers deal with breaking the rules.

High school faded into memory as college life came into focus. Cassie and I become kindreds in no time. We bonded through our sorority as we juggled classes, fulfilled pledge duties, and enjoyed active social lives, the latter of which sometimes meant going out, bar-hopping, and dancing with a group of friends. The legal drinking age for college students was lower back then, so if we chose to partake, at least we weren't breaking any laws.

Cassie and I chose to partake.

I've often told people I had a "typical freshman year." Growing up in a big college town and then going to school at another big college, it was almost a given that you'd at least try alcohol. Suddenly, you're away from home and you have absolute freedom to come and go and do as you please.

I came and went and did.

I shudder at some of my reckless choices my freshman year. Occasionally I was "overserved" and placed myself in foolish situations that could have brought me (or others) harm. More than once, I got behind the wheel after drinking. I was a shameless flirt and didn't think twice about being alone with a guy I considered a friend. I behaved as if I were invincible—no one would ever hurt me, and I wouldn't ever hurt anybody. (Absurd to me now.)

When I think about some of the choices I made back then, I can't help but thank God I didn't end up as one of those horrible headlines on the 11 o'clock news. I'm convinced that the prayers of my in-laws for their future daughter-in-law had something to do with it.

By my sophomore year, partying didn't have the allure it held just a year earlier. Truth be told, I had fun only about a quarter of the time. Most nights out were so-so or forgettable. Whatever I was looking for wasn't going to be found on the Bullwinkle's dance floor or at the bottom of a Budweiser.

About that same time, Cassie changed. She stopped drinking. I did my best to talk her out of the decision, but resolved, she explained her change of heart as graciously as she could. Her decision was linked to personal conviction flowing out of her relationship with Christ. She wasn't preaching at me or judging anyone else's choices. Her talk and walk radiated grace.

The obvious change in her lifestyle preached a powerful gospel. It had less to do with her not drinking, and more to do with how she reacted when everyone around her did: she loved—and liked—us all the same. There was no discernible difference in how she treated her friends who didn't share her same convictions.

There might not be a stronger visual for where we both were spiritually in this season than the night we were headed to a fraternity mixer just before Halloween. There wasn't a particular theme, so costumes could be anything. Cassie dressed as a baby doll—super sweet and innocent—and I decided on Jungle Jane, pretty much the exact opposite. I frizzed my hair and shimmied my way into a leopard-print, one-shoulder outfit on loan from a friend. Quite the pair, we decided to visit some hometown friends of hers on the way to the mixer, guys with whom she had gone to high school. They lived on E-3 in Johnstone, and their hall had remained almost intact from their freshman year.

By this point, Cassie's friends had become my friends, and these guys had seen us at our best . . . and worst. We must've been feeling pretty good about ourselves to bebop over in costume, and now that I think about it, Cassie had already been dating Robert for a while, an original E-3er from her hometown. It was hard not to notice us when we arrived on their hall. Most of the guys weren't in a fraternity and zero were in costume.

There is only one other thing I remember from this night: a glance.

I cannot tell you a single costume anyone else wore at the mixer or the fraternity who hosted that night. I don't know if we were the last to leave or the first to go. Did I drink hunch punch and dance on furniture or did I sip a Coke and shag to beach music with my friends? Who's to say? Better yet, who cares?

I can't remember anything except the E-3 resident assistant and I locking blue eyes to brown for half a second, and then a million butterflies unleashing in my stomach.

I had seen Tad plenty of times before, but he had always kept a cool distance, maybe because he had witnessed me in action my freshman year. I wasn't exactly the type of girl he was attracted to, so I'm not sure what changed for him that night. No doubt, something did. My wild mass of hair? The leopard print? If asked, I'm not sure he could give you an answer, outside the obvious Sunday school answer. *Jesus.* Thirty-plus years and three amazing kids later, He had to have been working in mysterious ways that night.

The short of the very long is Cassie did a little match-making and Tad and I started dating. Though neither of us recall the day of our first date—a regrettable lapse in memory—I know we saw *Stripes* at the Y theater on campus, and I did the "Rocky" victory dance at the top of the stairs. The latter made him rethink a second date, but he was wise enough not to share that little tidbit for years.

Tad wasn't like anyone I dated before, and the differences were both attractive and intimidating. He was serious about his faith and eager to encourage me in mine. He was the poster child for the Good Christian Guy—clean cut, a leader in high school youth group and Young Life, and he didn't drink, smoke, or cuss. His Bible sat on his desk and he didn't just read it, he studied it. He offered a handwritten list of Bible verses for me to memorize that spilled from the front side of a sheet of notebook paper to its back.

The guys I had dated in high school were from good families, and I'm sure they would have identified as Christian. But encouraging one another in our faith wasn't on our radar; I don't think we ever "considered how we might spur one another on toward love and good deeds" (Heb. 10:24 NIV). In contrast, Tad pointed me to God every way he could imagine. He introduced me to Keith Green, The Imperials, Amy Grant, and Dallas Holm. Discovering Christian music outside of traditional hymns or Sunday morning's *Gospel Jubilee* TV show introduced a freedom in worship I had never before experienced. You could have church music without a pipe organ? Who knew?

Cassie and Tad demonstrably lived their faith—with their words, in the choices they made, and by the way they treated other people. But there was also something very different about the way they talked about their faith, something that showed that they were living their faith on the *inside* too. It wasn't some pie-in-the-sky talk about a God we'll one day meet in heaven. This God they seemed to know so well was relational and accessible, abounding in love and generous with grace right here and right now. I understood the "performance" or outer way their faith was manifested, but this inner work was intriguing and new to me.

Their faith was personal. Intimate. On the *inside* and not just the outside. They found God to be caring like a friend, closer than a brother, loving, just, and wise like a good father. When they spoke of God, He wasn't distant. It was as if He were present with us, near because He wanted to be with the people He loved. This was a huge difference about Cassie and Tad—they showed me how outer behavior and inner faith could be aligned, that a person's faith can be *genuine* and not for show, approval, or brownie points. Their faith wasn't judgmental or condemning; it was appealing. Their faith was *real*.

As we spent more time together I realized they loved God because they knew Jesus—which is not the same thing as knowing *about* Jesus.

In their lives I was beginning to see how it's impossible to believe something you don't yet know, and that you can't really know someone you aren't spending time with (or haven't personally met).

It wasn't that they were perfect, but in a way that hadn't become clear to me quite yet, they were different in a good way. Eventually I'd come to understand this wasn't a night or day difference; it was the difference between life or death.

6

YOU DON'T KNOW WHAT YOU DON'T KNOW

Being ignorant is not so much a shame,
as being unwilling to learn.[8]
—Benjamin Franklin, *Poor Richard's Almanack*

I didn't learn what the Great Commission was until my sophomore year in college. That seems odd to me given how much time I spent at church and in faith-based activities throughout high school. How could I have missed that Jesus' call to action in Matthew 28 was commonly referred to as such?

> The eleven disciples traveled to Galilee, to the mountain where Jesus had directed them. When they saw him, they worshiped, but some doubted. Jesus came near and said to them, "All authority has been given to me in heaven and on earth. Go, therefore, and make disciples of all nations, baptizing them in the name of the Father and of the Son and of the Holy Spirit, teaching them to observe everything I have commanded you. And remember, I am with you always, to the end of the age." (Matt. 28:16–20)

While I had read this passage many times, I didn't know it was known as the Great Commission. How I discovered this lapse in knowledge was mortifying to me at the time.

I had joined a campus prayer breakfast where a few sororities and fraternities came together for a devotion, and to pray and share one morning a week. While the details are gloriously suppressed in my sub-sub-conscience, I know someone had brought up the Great Commission. However I responded must have made it abundantly clear I had no idea what he or she was talking about. I so wish I could tell you what I thought it meant then, what it was I had referenced. Chances are, it would make this story funnier or even more embarrassing.

The next time we met, one of our leaders casually began talking about the Matthew passage, carefully explaining the Great Commission in case "anyone didn't know what it was." The leader was careful not to bring up the previous week, and I wonder if anyone even remembered the discussion besides me.

As it became clear to me *exactly* for whom this lesson was planned, I could feel the heat rising up my neck and torching my cheeks. Though presented to the group, I knew they were correcting *my* misguided theology from the week prior. I was mortified. Of course they were being kind, trying to protect my dignity; but I knew, and at least some of them knew, and I felt like an idiot.

Did I realize I hadn't understood what the leader had been talking about? Had I simply made an educated guess or assumption based on the context of our conversation? If I was aware I didn't know, why couldn't I just admit it? Why did I feel pressure to pretend I knew more than I did (because we see how that turned out)? Was this all about my people-pleasing and wanting others to like me; fearing they wouldn't if I wasn't as Bible-literate as they were? Or was it, indeed, simply blissful ignorance?

Have you ever found yourself in Christian circles where it felt like everyone knew more than you? It's one thing if you've come to faith recently; everything is new and no one would expect you to have extensive knowledge about Scripture. But when you've grown up in the church, it can feel like you should know more than you do. And it's not so much external pressure from others; we do this to ourselves. It's one more way the comparison game can assault our heart. Why do we feel pressure to feel like we're supposed to know it all?

If the Great Commission debacle wasn't enough to drown me in a sea of insecurity, there was also the first time I met Tad's parents.

We had been dating for a while, serious enough to warrant a parental introduction. We planned a visit from college but I grew increasingly anxious as the weekend drew near. I knew Tad had talked to them about me and my mostly-former woolly ways, and I wondered if they would judge me or worry about me corrupting their son. They hadn't known me the way the community of my youth had known me, as a church-going, people-pleasing good girl. If they caught wind of some of the regrettable decisions I had made in the past few years, there was no "aw honey, she's just going through a phase—Robin's always been a good girl since she was little" explanation to fall back on. All they knew was the college version of me. Always the pleaser, I was concerned they wouldn't accept me because of some of the poorer choices I had made.

Thankfully, my fears were unfounded. Tommy and Sarah received me with open arms literally and figuratively from the moment we met, and their home offered comfort by way of acceptance . . . and food.

Sarah's cooking was legendary and no one in their right mind would decline an invitation for a meal. Always tended with care and intention, her table was a book you actually could judge by its cover. She believed fine china and silver weren't treasures to be buried away in boxes, but holy vessels with the power to transform an everyday meal into something special. Sarah wasn't just practicing hospitality when she used her Haviland and sterling; without a word she was telling you how glad she was to have you at her table. You knew it, too. You felt it.

As a college student subsisting on bland, starchy, and uninspired dining hall fare, I suddenly found myself in a magical place where all the dishes were the best of their kind. I was shoveling it in so fast Sarah exclaimed, "I'm so glad Tad is dating someone who eats!" I cringe to think I must've looked like every bite was my last. Though I was embarrassed at first, she genuinely meant it as a compliment. Time would teach me that people filling their plates with seconds and thirds is high praise to the cook.

It was during Sunday lunch I put my ignorance on display once again, going on a fishing expedition to try to learn more about Tad's family's faith. It was impossible not to notice something different about them, and I mean that in a good way: they spoke about God as if they knew Him personally. They were so familiar, in fact, it wouldn't have surprised me if Jesus had shown up at their table any second to join us. It was the same sort of difference I had been noticing in Tad and Cassie, though I was still learning what that meant.

I asked the most logical question I knew that might provide insight into "who" they were spiritually:

"What religion are y'all?"

Without missing a beat, Tommy and Sarah, and maybe even Tad, chimed in—"You mean *denomination*?"—and I felt stupid all over again, because yes, that's what I meant, but I didn't know how to ask until I heard them say it.

I have little recollection of how they answered because the blood rushing to my ears sounded like Niagara Falls, drowning out their voices and dousing my pride. They didn't think twice about it, but that didn't stop me from clobbering myself silly with hammers of condemnation. For some reason I felt like I was supposed to know *everything* about Christianity by virtue of my Southern birth and since I had gone to church practically every Sunday since I was born. There's no worse moment for a church-raised girl than to realize she doesn't, in fact, have a clue.

These are trivial examples from a lifetime ago but they illustrate a point: You don't know what you don't know. There is absolutely no shame in that, either. To master any subject or skill, there's a learning curve. Depending on the complexity of the material, craft, hobby, or sport, it could take years of study or practice to become knowledgeable, proficient, and/or accomplished. Even then, there's always room to improve or learn more.

> You don't know what you don't know. There is absolutely no shame in that.

Michael Phelps, the most decorated Olympian of all time, didn't win gold the first time he jumped in a pool. He learned how to swim when he was seven, began training with a coach at eleven, and qualified for his first Olympics when he was fifteen. Medals would begin pouring in four years later; six gold, two bronze. His event times broke both world and Olympic records. Phelps didn't win twenty-eight Olympic medals and hundreds of elite competitions just by hanging out in the water. He deliberately studied as much as he could about his sport and then swam a million miles. Simple steps in theory, but in practice, it was mentally and physically demanding.

Simply growing up in the church doesn't guarantee that we remember, internalize, or even understand everything we once heard or learned. There were plenty of things I "learned" as a church kid that I currently have zero recollection of—and even if I remembered what to say or do as a child, it wasn't born out of a true love for God. Now, I'm not advocating for parents to stop teaching their children Scripture and the principles that flow from it. We should all teach our kids truth from God's Word, and yes, the knowledge they build has the potential to help them in the future when they do become believers.

However, I *am* saying that abiding faith doesn't occur by osmosis or accident or even by rote memorization. Simply growing up in church won't create the genuine faith I saw in Cassie and Tad and his parents.

Instead, upon conversion, the Holy Spirit inhabits our being and becomes our Helper—He helps us remember the things we would naturally forget if left to ourselves. That's His part in the deal. But our part matters too.

Abiding faith doesn't occur by osmosis or accident or even by rote memorization.

In order to strengthen our relationship with God, we can't be passive. Growing in intimacy comes primarily by reading His Word and spending time in prayer. You know this, I know this, and yet apparently we need reminders. As we engage in prayer and His Word, the Spirit continues its transforming work, making us more like Christ. Yes, we are doing some "outer" work that others can see, like participating in spiritual disciplines, but this is supposed to be paired with the Spirit's "inner" work—granting us genuine faith and real love for God. When we encounter God in this balanced way (instead of only engaging in the outer work, my more typical go-to back then), it brings change—healing, maturity, and a clearer understanding of His will and His ways (though much will remain a mystery this side of heaven).

Doing our part to grow in the knowledge of God only happens by discipline and study, not because we simply want to know more. Good intentions don't get us there. Nor can we rely only on the felt board Bible stories we heard over and over as a child.

Never have I wished more for SciFi to be reality than when Neo, Keanu Reeve's character in the 1999 film *The Matrix*, learned everything there was to know about jiu-jitsu in five seconds. Seriously, upload a program through some magical computer thingy straight to your brain and you're mentally and physically proficient? Yes, please.

We know how far-fetched Neo's experience is, so why do we expect learning about God to be just like it? Why do we place unrealistic expectations on ourselves to know more than we do, or to know everything in five seconds (or in a couple years of high school or college ministry or a Sunday morning sermon or a six-week Bible study)?

Maybe it was the church kid in me, but in adulthood, part of me believed that being a lifelong Christian meant I was not only supposed to know a lot more than I did, but that I was supposed to know it all overnight; it's illogical, but it's the only explanation for why I still vividly remember how I felt in the two examples I shared.

Why did I feel stupid (or think that's how others would view me) when I was mistaken about what the Great Commission meant? According to a 2018 Barna study in partnership with the Seed Company, 51 percent of churchgoers didn't know the term and 25 percent were familiar but didn't know the exact meaning. Only 17 percent could tell you what it meant![9] I realize the data would be different thirty years ago, but you get the picture. I'm sure I was still in the majority.

I don't know what the things are in your life that you feel like you should know by now but don't, or examples where your ignorance about a subject was revealed in a public way, but it bears repeating: *you don't know what you don't know* and there is no shame in that. Shame is one of those destructive forces, like fear, that has no place in the kingdom of God. It is one of those "schemes of the devil" and "flaming arrows" referred to in Ephesians 6:10–20:

> Finally, be strengthened by the Lord and by his vast strength. Put on the full armor of God so that you can stand against the schemes of the devil. For our struggle is not against flesh and blood, but against the rulers, against the authorities, against the cosmic powers of this darkness, against evil, spiritual forces in the heavens. For this reason take up the full armor of God, so that you may be able to resist in the evil day, and having prepared everything, to take your stand. Stand, therefore, with truth like a belt around your waist, righteousness like armor on your chest,

and your feet sandaled with readiness for the gospel of peace. In every situation take up the shield of faith with which you can extinguish all the flaming arrows of the evil one. Take the helmet of salvation and the sword of the Spirit—which is the word of God. Pray at all times in the Spirit with every prayer and request, and stay alert with all perseverance and intercession for all the saints. Pray also for me, that the message may be given to me when I open my mouth to make known with boldness the mystery of the gospel. For this I am an ambassador in chains. Pray that I might be bold enough to speak about it as I should.

Shame is dangerous because it shifts focus from God to ourselves and inflicts heart damage. What a subtle ploy of our enemy. It would be easier if our struggle *was* against flesh and blood; we could see it coming and measure the collateral damage. When you're dealing with "evil" or "spiritual forces," you can't fight on your own, not effectively, anyway. Goodness knows I've tried. It's like treading water in quicksand—exhausting and going nowhere fast.

Sometimes we simply don't know what we don't know. All we should do in that situation is to keep moving forward in our walk with God, and trust that the Lord will show us what we need to know as we go. But other times we *do* know and have either forgotten or don't care. But that's an entirely different story.

7

HAMSTER WHEELS

If you don't know where you're going,
any road will get you there.[10]
—George Harrison, "Any Road"

When I was a teen, our church's youth group was small and about the farthest thing from cool it could be. Our leaders had no hip glasses or trendy facial hair, no Untuckit shirts, no flip-flops. No fog machine, no Xbox, not even a foosball table. It wasn't flashy, but we met every week to spend time in the Word, play a few games, and consider how to serve our church body.

Maybe not any flashier but decidedly more cool, the Fellowship of Christian Athletes assembled church-going students into one big, fat ecumenical family. As a high school cheerleader, I qualified for FCA membership (not that there was an actual membership). Each week during the school year, athletes and non-athletes alike gathered in a musty, musky weight room to hang out, watch skits, and listen to a coach deliver a short devotion.

Both were good clean fun that did the double-duty of keeping teens out of trouble and providing opportunity to hear the gospel and to grow in our faith. The thing is, I had already heard and responded to the gospel, and growing in my faith was a secondary concern to the real reason my attendance was so consistent: to spend time with my friends and to flirt with boys. Oh, I would have never admitted it then, but I was more interested in socializing than getting to know Jesus better.

I'm a Baby Boomer by the skin of my teeth. Coming of age in the late '70s and '80s was different than in today's world; a "good girl" mentality still existed. Judeo-Christian values were normative regardless of religious affiliation. The pressure wasn't only from home or church to abstain from drinking, smoking, drug use, profanity, or having sex, it was the general ethos of our culture. No doubt, plenty of monkeyshines were going on, but at least we mentally assented to the values of our parents.

Our social networks were face to face or at their most distant, a landline connected to a corded telephone. No—wait—pen pals. Pen pals connected us to exotic new friends across the country or the world. Nothing compared to getting to know a new friend by reading her hand-written, three-page letter. We never had to worry that some creepy man in his underwear, squirreled away in the corner of a dimly-lit basement, might be the one writing back.

We were connected in meaningful ways that required us actually to have met in person (pen pals the exception). The word *friend* was always a noun, never a verb. If we were friends, we had an honest-to-goodness relationship built over time and because we were either drawn to each other by natural affection, common interests, or geographical proximity.

Having attended public school my whole life, denominational diversity among my friends was common; for the most part, we all attended different churches. There wasn't one cool church or youth group that attracted the masses. I doubt the word "cool" was ever attached to anything church-related at all. You attended the youth group of the church you belonged to, and unlike my own children, you didn't attend a different youth group just because all your friends went there.

My college years ushered in a new season in my faith, where I began to understand a much broader picture of God by getting to know Jesus. Even saying the name "Jesus" was new to me; it brought with it an intimacy that, if I'm honest, made me a little uncomfortable. I still enjoyed socializing when I attended church and Bible studies, but I was eager to learn and grow in my faith. It was hard juggling all that—school, sorority (officer responsibilities kept me hopping), boyfriend—and I was sure it would get easier once I graduated.

Then I graduated.

Tad and I weren't ready for marriage, so he headed one way and I went the other. The other took me to Atlanta. He worked a while and eventually returned to school to complete a double major, and I found a job and pretty much wandered in circles the next two years. During that time, I attended several different Bible studies and visited a number of churches with friends. Right around when I had finally settled on a church to join, Tad and I decided to get married.

After a brief stint living and working near the beach, we settled into jobs and life in South Carolina, becoming members of the first church we visited, happy with it from Day One. For the next several years we plugged in, joining a newly-formed adult Sunday school class and attending Wednesday night supper and Bible study. We served on committees and volunteered for our church's mercy ministries and outreach. We showed up for church-wide events. After I gave birth to our first daughter, I accepted a position on church staff. As we matured, our roles and service matured, and if the church doors were open, we were there. Not out of some misguided sense of obligation, but because Westminster had become our church home—a community of people we loved and with whom we delighted in doing life together. We were all in.

I was all in at Westminster Presbyterian Church the same way I had been all in my youth group and FCA, and more faith-based groups and associations than is necessary to detail. You get the point. Each group or class or association or community provided opportunity to learn, grow, serve, receive, and give.

Needs were being met, mine and others. Lives were impacted. I scaled mountaintops and trudged valleys.

I could check most, if not all, of the Christian boxes. Consistent church attendance. Serving others. Bible study, tithing, even the more obscure service like helping on the cookbook committee and redesigning our weekly church bulletin. I even prepared a complicated Greek dish for a competition during our International Missions Festival and won a trophy.

What were my motives? No doubt, age, stage of life, and circumstances impacted my choices. What compelled me to action at sixteen would've been very different at thirty-six. At any point could I honestly say I was driven by my love for God so deeply I was compelled to follow Him into those places? Was my overriding concern to know Him so intimately that my life was conspicuously different than the world and culture surrounding me, that others might see Him in me and leave my presence wanting more of Christ? Was it to know God and make Him known?

I hope at least sometimes. But mostly I was on a hamster wheel, spinning the same old circle, doing and performing and striving toward imaginary Christian expectations and ideals. There is never a shortage of opportunity to serve in a church, that's for sure. But that doesn't mean you (or I) have to say "yes" to every one of them. Sometimes a "yes" to a good thing precludes God's best for us had we said no.

> Sometimes a "yes" to a good thing precludes God's best for us had we said no.

It's tempting sometimes to look at those years and my efforts with contempt. I have spent too much time missing the Kingdom over and over again by the proverbial eighteen inches that I've mentioned before—the distance between my head and heart. But contempt isn't a dialect of the Lord; it's an effective tool of our enemy to shift focus from God to myself.

Satan is so good at what he does. Smoke and mirrors. Divide and conquer. Whittling away our hearts into tiny splinters so we don't even realize he's the one at work. If I'm so busy banging my head against the wall for my shortcomings or short-sightedness—beating myself up for not knowing what I didn't know—I could miss what God has for me despite myself or my misguided motives. He's still at work. He's still for me. He's called me, forgiven me, and He's praying for me. *God is praying for us.* God's patience toward His children is a mystery to me, but I'm thankful.

Those churchy things we do aren't bad in and of themselves. In fact they provide a lot of good for a lot of people. They teach us about God. They place us in a position to learn about the history of our faith and to serve others.

But only when a hamster steps off his wheel can he actually get anywhere. Makes you wonder why they stay on so long.

8

MOUNTAINS AND VALLEYS

God's sovereignty is unpredictable.
We must always trust Him even
when we don't understand.[11]
—Dr. Tony Evans

My daughter lives in Denver, Colorado, just twelve miles east of the Rocky Mountain foothills. Aptly nicknamed the Mile High City due to its one-mile-above-sea-level elevation, on a clear day the views are startling. When we visit—if the weather isn't being a jerk—we always plan a hike. It's one of the reasons we can tolerate Rachel living so far away from us.

Hiking in the Rockies is a different animal than hiking their eastern cousin, the Appalachians (the range closest to where I've always lived). Depending on the trails you choose, Rocky Mountain climbs can be twice the elevation. The air is thinner, making it harder to breathe. Dehydration can sneak up on you.

Before our first hike there, we were well informed about what to expect and how to respond to the differences in altitude and elevation change. Yet just fifteen minutes into my first Rocky Mountain hike, theory slipped out of my head and into my lungs.

I was wrong to think being in good shape was enough to handle the trail; I couldn't catch my breath. But this felt different from becoming winded by physical exertion; we hadn't been walking that fast or that far before I became light-headed and nauseous. It was unfamiliar and unnerving. No, more than that . . . downright scary. Realizing I was no longer in sight, Tad and Rachel backtracked to find me with my head tucked between my knees trying to pace my breathing, steady my nerves, and stave off tears. I wondered if this was what it felt like to suffocate or drown. Though a bit melodramatic, my borderline-ridiculous thoughts were an indication how difficult it was to breathe. Suspecting my age contributed to my body betraying me added insult to injury.

Gradually, thankfully, my breathing acclimated to the altitude and we were able to continue without further incident. That first and subsequent hikes have introduced me to some of the most beautiful spectacles on earth—emerald lakes reminiscent of fairy tales, cotton-capped peaks under impossibly blue skies, and dazzling views that tried their best to cure my lifelong battle with acrophobia.

There was a cost of admission, though, beyond my early-onset respiratory issue. Afterwards, muscles hurt I didn't even know I had. The more challenging trails required persistence, endurance, and mental and physical agility. My body's frailty and limitations were exposed. With every trek, I'd walk away with a deeper respect and greater appreciation for the Rockies.

The terrain of life can be just as impactful to our faith, can't it? All of us face our share of mountains, valleys, peaks, and ordinary days. Each one is formative in life and faith, uniquely significant and equally valuable. We're shaped by the circumstances, pressures, and influences around us. To try and resist this reality is futile. Change is inevitable. We might as well embrace it.

Isn't it funny how day by day nothing changes, but when we look back, everything is different?[12]

Whether a molehill or the Matterhorn, a mountain can stop you in your tracks. Mountains disrupt status quo and future plans. They require you to expend energy on something you hadn't expected, something that wasn't in the blueprint. Mountains divert the route you're on and insist you take a detour. There are options as to how you'll get to the other side of each mountain. Some you climb. Others, you must go around. And sometimes they're so large you have to tuck your chin, buckle your seat belt, and tunnel straight through.

Personal mountains are things that happen *to* you, things outside of your control that get inserted in your life without your permission. They can look like a lot of things: job stress or unemployment, an unexpected financial setback that wasn't due to your own irresponsibility, or general uncertainties about the future. Marital or relational discord, disconnect, or infidelity. The never-ending challenges of raising children. A season of life you wish you could finally get out of. An unexpected rift in a friendship. A betrayal you never saw coming. A frightening diagnosis.

The way I'm looking at it, mountains are born of external circumstances, while valleys are largely an interior battle in the mind or heart. I've typically viewed valleys as the things that happen *in* you. They can be rivers of sorrow and sadness, depression or despair, gloomy days, a long, endless night. They can look like unbelief, bitterness, or a past sin-struggle that resurfaces out of nowhere. Valleys may be a result of a newly emerged mountain, and they are often connected to people—broken trust, unresolved conflict, estranged relationships. You can become paralyzed in the valley, barely able to go through the motions of life. Right foot, left foot, breathe in, breathe out . . . sometimes that's the best you can do.

The worst part of a valley is feeling alone and isolated. You desperately need others but it's hard to ask for help. Perhaps you've been wounded so deeply you don't feel safe and you've lost the ability to trust others. Maybe your valley is tied to addiction or secret sin, and you're unwilling to disappoint or alienate those closest to you. You're collapsing under a weight of grief or shame or inadequacy.

When facing mountains or going through valleys we bargain with God, we dig for joy, we beg and weep, we shake our fist and curse. We pray for wisdom, relief, grace, and deliverance. We mine the Scriptures for truth, power, answers, and sometimes, though we'd be slow to see or admit it, we even try to earn God's favor. Won't God bless us if we only do our part? Or, for others of us, maybe those mountains and valleys bring us to the edge of our faith and instead of trying harder, we're ready to chuck it all and say good riddance to religion altogether.

Here's what I've learned time and again—something you've probably learned over and over as well. It's a lesson we all know from experience but have difficulty remembering in the heat of a trial: never do we grow more spiritually—never does our character mature more—than when we endure an extended hard season.

> Never do we grow more spiritually—never does our character mature more—than when we endure an extended hard season.

Mountains and valleys strengthen our faith muscles. They expand our capacity to one, believe God no matter what, and two, empathize with and extend compassion to others. Until you've walked in a particular pair of shoes, you cannot understand how they feel.

Paul describes it this way in 2 Corinthians 1:4–5: "[God] comforts us in all our affliction, so that we may be able to comfort those who are in any kind of affliction, through the comfort we ourselves receive from God. For just as the sufferings of Christ overflow to us, so also through Christ our comfort overflows."

> We can always look behind us to see the faithfulness of God, even if we didn't recognize it en route.

Our experiences are never wasted. When we reach the far side of the valley or mountain, we've gained something of great value in the process—new insight, wisdom, understanding, and the confidence that comes from standing on the other side. We can always look behind us to see the faithfulness of God, even if we didn't recognize it en route.

And another beautiful takeaway? All that we've learned is rarely intended for us to keep to ourselves.

Our mountains and valleys always bear testimony to God's faithfulness. And I know, *I know,* when tragedy strikes, it is almost impossible to sense God's goodness, to believe He has your best interest at heart. This is what gives me the brightest hope during those bleakest moments: I don't have to feel God's faithfulness to me for it to be true, I don't even have to believe it. The same way it doesn't matter whether or not I believe in gravity; if I drop a rock, it's going to fall down, not remain suspended in mid-air or float up. What is true, is true, regardless of what I think or feel. God's truth isn't dependent on my understanding, my actions, or even my level of trust or faithfulness in any given moment. When we can't make sense of our lives, and when it seems like God should turn His back on us because

> I don't have to feel God's faithfulness to me for it to be true.

we've been struggling to trust Him, Isaiah 55:8–9 offers an important reminder: "'For my thoughts are not your thoughts, and your ways are not my ways.' This is the LORD's declaration. 'For as heaven is higher than earth, so my ways are higher than your ways, and my thoughts than your thoughts.'" God doesn't work the way we do. He stays faithful even in the places we wouldn't. Aren't you thankful?

After I had given birth to my youngest, a friend at full-term gave birth to a stillborn son. It was devastating and our entire church community circled close. Heartbroken, I felt a (false) sense of guilt for delivering three healthy babies, and inadequate for not knowing what to say or do. I'll never forget how my friend Beth encouraged me when I told her

I couldn't begin to imagine what our friend was feeling and I had no idea how to help. "There's no way you can understand. You haven't had to learn what this feels like by going through the same thing yourself. We aren't all created to experience life or minister to others in the exact same ways . . ."

These were new thoughts to me, profound even, piggy-backing on Paul's words in 2 Corinthians. Beth wasn't absolving me of praying for or caring about my friend; but she was releasing me from trying to feel something impossible for me to feel. This hadn't been my particular cup to bear, but those who had experienced a similar loss knew how best to comfort and encourage this mama. Put another way, we are able to offer comfort and empathy as a result of what we've received by way of experience.

Mountains and valleys are powerful forces in our lives because they test our limits, bring us to the end of ourselves, and reveal our desperate need for God. And though no one is eager for obstacles to surface (nor should we go seeking misery just for the sake of it), Scripture provides an excellent lens for how to view them:

> Consider it a great joy, my brothers and sisters, whenever you experience various trials, because you know that the testing of your faith produces endurance. And let endurance have its full effect, so that you may be mature and complete, lacking nothing. (James 1:2–4)

Endurance leading to maturity is a by-product of tested faith. It is why we're able to consider trials a "great joy"; not in a disingenuous "I'm so happy to find myself in a living nightmare right now" sort of way, but realizing that holy and hard work is taking place to conform us to the image of Christ.

Yes, much is expected of the believer who finds herself standing at the foot of a mountain or the valley's entrance. God didn't give us legs to just stand there, look up or out, and gawk at the immensity of the terrain. He made us to climb, to take the next step, to move! Even if you can't see the other side or the end, it is there waiting. Time always reveals what is uncertain today.

Take heart, Wanderer: mountains and valleys come and go. Where you are today is not where you'll be forever. Sometimes you need someone to remind you of that.

9

OPPORTUNITY LOST

Footfalls echo in the memory
Down the passage which we did not take
Towards the door we never opened.[13]
—T. S. Eliot, "Burnt Norton"

We had been married just fifteen months and already we were on our second move. Although our new hometown brought us closer to family, we were still hours away from friends or relatives. We were eager to put down roots and start meeting people. Our dance card was empty and begging its fill.

As fate would have it, opportunity came quickly and conveniently. Barely were our own boxes emptied and broken down when, lo and behold, we noticed someone moving in below us. Employing some mighty impressive sleuthing skills—spying out the kitchen window—I deduced that they looked a lot like us, twenty-somethings with no kids. I made brownies the next week, marched downstairs, and knocked on the door. To my delight, brownies were one of Christi's love languages, too. There is no sweeter foundation for friendship than a shared love of chocolate.

We chatted a few minutes and covered the basics—her husband was starting a new job and she was looking for one, just like Tad and me—and we exchanged names and numbers. This was in the late '80s, so we were stuck with landlines and, you know, actually having to call and talk to one another in order to make plans. We picked a date for them to come over for dinner soon after. Friendship was already looking promising.

Getting to know new people can be awkward, even for those who are outgoing and friendly by nature. Though it's easier when you're all in the same boat—strangers in a new town was just the beginning of our similarities—there are still those clumsy moments when you're grasping for something of interest to add to the conversation without accidentally stepping onto a land mine that will bring the evening to an abrupt and blistering end. In other words, until you and I have established a safe, healthy relationship where we've learned we might have to agree to disagree sometimes, there are topics I'd be a fool to bring up. Whether or not you squeeze and crimp your toothpaste, if you're acquainted with the correct way to hang toilet paper (over, not under), climate change, politics . . . religion. For a first get-together, I wanted to play it nice and vanilla—don't forget I was a card-carrying people-pleaser—so I treaded lightly as I got to know this new couple.

We were on dessert when Frankie asked a question that revealed something about both of us. "So, you guys play tennis?" I couldn't imagine what gave him that idea. Though we may have picked up a racquet off and on through the years, I could think of nothing in our apartment that would indicate such a thing.

My brow furrowed into a question, and I smiled, inviting explanation as I shook my head and said, "No . . . ?" Frankie pointed to the books on our mantel and continued, "I figured at least one of you must play since you have a book called *Improving Your Serve* . . . ?"[14] Squirmy and concerned we might come across as Jesus freaks, I mumbled something about it being a book related to Christian servanthood and then quickly moved the conversation along.

The night went well enough that Christi and Frankie reciprocated with a dinner invitation at their place, a volley that continued for years.

Christi and I would end up finding jobs within a week of each other. When each of us bought our first houses the next year, we excitedly helped the other move. Her daughter was born nine months after mine, and we'd continue taking turns having babies so they stair-stepped in school (and even matched genders). We hosted and attended baby showers for one another. We could navigate each other's kitchens and I thought it was a Divine Stamp of Approval that we had sister Lenox patterns for everyday dishes (me, Poppies on Blue; her, Glories on Grey). We discovered we had the same pencil post bed and Laura Ashley bedding (Bembridge, for those with a need to know such things). We vacationed together with and without kids, and though we haven't lived in the same town for over fifteen years, Christi has never missed sending a birthday card to both of us. (I'm afraid I might not have that strong of a track record.)

Without meaning to, and worse, not realizing it, I once hurt Christi's feelings. When she finally summoned the nerve to confront me about it, I was flabbergasted and heartbroken to have been oblivious to the pain I caused (her point was valid). Our friendship was rooted in love and respect, and I was thankful it mattered enough to her to deal with my offense, and take the necessary steps to get things out in the open so we could make things right.

Inevitably, life and friendship got more complicated with job and kids and subsequent moves even farther away from each other. But, because ours is still a friendship punctuated by commas when we part company, we're able to pick up right where we left off the last time we finagled a visit.

After a grand season of doing life together, and decades of knowing and loving one another, I am still bothered by my response to Frankie that first time they came for dinner, when he asked about us playing tennis. It sounds ludicrous, even to me, that so small a thing would occupy any space at all in my memory; I can't even remember what I wore yesterday, for goodness sake. My theory as to why has evolved through the years, tangled up in half of a verse in the New Testament, and the heart of an oft-repeated quote attributed to Maya Angelou:

> For I am not ashamed of the gospel, because it is the power of God for salvation to everyone who believes. . . . For in it the righteousness of God is revealed from faith to faith, just as it is written: The righteous will live by faith. (Rom. 1:16–17)

> "I've learned that people will forget what you said, people will forget what you did, but people will never forget how you made them feel."[15]

It's important to be clear: it was not our new friend who caused this event to be seared in my memory. As a tennis player and fan, it was logical for him to think he might have discovered a natural connection. However, it was my response (or more accurately, my non-response) that pinched a nerve. Hard. How I made *myself* feel. In a very real sense the way I responded suggested, at least to me, I was ashamed of the gospel. Instead of stepping through a door of opportunity to share my faith, I turned and walked the other way. Teed up perfectly, I whiffed the ball.

No one else may have known it, but I did.

Maybe it seems like I'm too hard on myself, that it's ridiculous to have had existential angst over something so seemingly small. But in my own heart, I know God was convicting me. It's important to understand that conviction is very different than condemnation (Rom. 8:1)—God was certainly not condemning me! But the truth is, I made a misstep, God convicted me about it, and this is a good thing. When I make a wrong move in my faith, the first step in correction is realizing what I've done. We're going to have slip-ups in this thing called the Christian life, and it's best to admit when we do. Conviction is God's way of letting us know when we're about to stumble or are already in sin, and though it stings, it's a gift.

Missed opportunities related to my faith weren't limited to a single incident. At the same time friendship with our neighbors was developing, so was life in our church. When a new adult Sunday school class was formed not long after we arrived, we jumped at the chance to become a part. With the hope of encouraging its members to love others the way God loves us—unconditionally and without bounds—it was named Agape, a "same age and stage" kind of couple's class. When it launched, with the exception of our leaders, none of the members had children. Most of us worked full-time, and we had the freedom and time to invest in relationships without the additional demands of little people underfoot.

Once again, we were all in. We had frequent class get-togethers and didn't miss on Sunday mornings if at all possible. We'd have each other over for dinner. We served and we served and we served because we wanted to demonstrate our love for each other, our church, and our community. We set aside time for an annual retreat that included teaching from someone outside our class but also plenty of free time for bonding. Because we were logging time together, relationships were taking root and flourishing.

It was such a sweet time in our lives. We were a group of young adults beginning to navigate real life, optimistic about what the future would hold and doing all we could to grow in our faith. We were busy serving together, eating together, and growing in our love for God together. We also must've been drinking from the same cup, because soon every Sunday brought with it a pregnancy announcement.

We continued doing life together, and what that meant exactly expanded over time. For years our class was a steady stream of mostly good news—pregnancies and births—hosting baby showers, and making and taking meals to parents of newborns. But we also tenderly carried one another when tragedy arrived at the door . . . infertility, miscarriage, an ill parent, job loss. We were all in, indeed.

Tad and I were thankful to have a solid friendship outside of church with our neighbors (who attended a different church), but otherwise our closest friendships were born in the Agape class. I suppose it was inevitable that eventually we'd grow closer to some couples at a deeper level than others. And, unfortunately, *that* created some problems when a tight-knit group of us traveled out of town together, leaving noticeable absences in our class on the Sunday mornings we were gone.

Feelings were hurt. Accusations were hurled. People felt excluded. And today I would handle it differently than I did all those years ago. Or at least I think and hope I would.

Though I could justify these get-aways with friends, even biblically, the truth is I was experiencing a *missed* opportunity to love others more than myself. Galatians 5:13–14 tells us, "For you were called to be free, brothers and sisters; only don't use this freedom as an opportunity for the flesh, but serve one another through love. For the whole law is fulfilled in one statement: *Love your neighbor as yourself*" (emphasis added). I was asserting my rights, my freedom, my flesh, over perhaps the more right thing to do. I could have looked for more ways to include all class members in deepening our friendships with one another. We could have returned home in time to be at church on Sunday mornings so there wasn't a large gap in attendance. I could have foregone the trip altogether. There were any number of choices I could have made as a more loving thing to do once I learned my actions were hurting others.

Hear me on this—there is absolutely nothing wrong about a group of friends going away for the weekend; friendships can grow deeper as special memories are made together. But, in our case, wonderful memories came at a cost to others (and likely myself), and that grieves me.

Though these experiences were years before the worst of my wander years, I was making missteps along the way (mostly unaware), just like anyone does as they try to navigate friendship and church and family. As I peer in the rearview mirror though, I can't help but wonder what other chances have passed me by to share or live out my faith, to introduce Jesus to those who might not know Him, to love others more than myself? For every lost opportunity, I'm so grateful for a faithful God who is patiently waiting to be found, who offers course correction when I step off my path, and who brings conviction that leads to repentance.

10

PATTERNS AND PRACTICE

It is never too soon to prepare for the rest of our lives.[16]
—Jean Fleming, *Pursue the Intentional Life*

It hadn't taken me long to receive a job offer after arriving in South Carolina. In a world with no online résumé builders or job-finding websites, I went about it the the the old-fashioned way: sending out neatly typed résumés along with personal cover letters. Focusing on the industry I worked for in Atlanta and firms large enough to require a corporate marketing department, I mass-mailed—*snail*-mailed—a dozen companies I had identified from a Chamber of Commerce directory. I was throwing spaghetti noodles against the wall, and thankfully a good one stuck.

I accepted a job as marketing coordinator for a large general contracting firm. The only downside I could point to was a forty-minute commute and city traffic, but I loved my boss, and learned a lot from her; on top of that, I enjoyed our entire team.

About a year later I was hardly looking for a job when I was approached to become the marketing director for Westminster Towers, a continuing care retirement community right in my backyard. My pastor and the elder overseeing the adult Sunday school class we attended were both board members, and they presented a job description that sounded too good to be true. Following weeks of conversation, negotiation, and prayer, I finally accepted their offer, leaving behind a job I liked for the idealistic hope of making a real difference in the lives of those I would now be serving. It never occurred to me that I would, in fact, be walking into a classroom for life. While I valued it as a well-suited job fit marrying together my education, experience, and most important, natural affection for the age group with whom I'd be working, I didn't expect to learn anything. I'm not sure if my short-sightedness was due to arrogance or the obliviousness of youth.

As marketing director, my primary role was to sell independent living apartments to retirees who required no assistance, with a million secondary responsibilities to support this main objective. I understood from the outset that building relationships with the existing residents was integral to my success. They had the potential to be goodwill ambassadors for our community, walking and talking billboards that could make—or break—a sale. Every prospect tour included a visit to one of our resident's apartments, the choice of which was always carefully curated and calculated. A Nellie Naysayer could torpedo half a dozen positive interactions with residents. One single, careless, negative remark might kill a sale.

It was at Westminster Towers I first learned to appreciate the depth of life hidden beneath the surface of who we are. Especially when you're young, it's so easy to cross paths with an octogenarian and only see "old." It's not a conscious practice; we're likely unaware when it happens. But it does happen, and what a disservice on both sides. Every gray hair, each line that carves a face, is earned and paid for with time. To reach old age—and I realize that's relative—is to have lived a thousand stories, to have survived a thousand more. As multi-dimensional beings passing through time and space, our days write a chapter, and those chapters account for one extraordinary book.

Our residents were always happy to share some of their thousands of stories with me, eager even, and I discovered that listening could be a gift in and of itself. Had I not had work to do, and had the wisdom to take advantage of the great wealth of experience surrounding me, I would have asked more questions.

Still, my retirement community observations taught me a valuable lesson: With each day we become more of who we are.

Mr. Higgins was my favorite "teacher." For that matter, he might have been everyone's favorite. He was a ninety-something gentleman, neat, frail, and determined in the softest of ways. The gravity of his kindness was inescapable, and his eyes never stopped twinkling. One day I was headed to join my coworkers for lunch when he decided to make my day—"You're just about the prettiest thing I've ever seen." His generous remark lifted my spirits and sent me walking on air.

When I arrived at lunch still on a Mr. Higgins cloud, I told my colleagues about our exchange. Our often grumpy director of nursing brought me down to earth lickety-split—"You *do* know he's legally blind and he can't actually see you, right?" Well, hmph. Mr. Higgins' superpowers were so strong his compliment lingered anyway.

Mrs. Pierce was my favorite, too. She was thoughtful and practical, loyal and resourceful. Plus, she could've been Harper Lee's sister right down to her pageboy and glasses. We worked together on the resident newsletter committee, and I could count on her like clockwork. She meant business with her yeses, which taught me to respect her nos. She valued people and quietly served everyone around her, keeping her eyes open for any opportunity, every need. She noticed what others missed, and I noticed her noticing.

It's easy to gush madly about the dear friends I made at Westminster Towers—Mr. Higgins and Mrs. Pierce are two of many—but you might imagine there were residents who were a wee bit harder to love, like, or sometimes even tolerate. They found tiny dark clouds in otherwise blue skies. Fractious or demanding, impossible to please, or sometimes downright mean, they sucked the air right out of the room.

I wondered about these folks in particular. What had skewed their perspective to always see a half-empty glass? Why were they so negative compared to their positive, half-full-glass neighbors? It hit me that my older friends really weren't necessarily that different from my contemporaries—I wasn't just surrounded by half-full/half-empty glass people at work. Most people have a smattering of both in their lives, and I was no different.

But then an even greater realization occurred to me: the older we get the more we become like we already are. Kind people become more kind. Generous people give even more freely. Grumpy people become grumpier. And those with unreasonable demands will never be pleased.

> The older we get the more we become like we already are.

Then it got personal. I realized that I was on the way to becoming more of who I am. Who was it I wanted to become?

I discovered Jean Fleming's important book, *Pursue the Intentional Life,* years later, and she articulated perfectly what I had observed in my position at the retirement community—

> The truth is that everyone, regardless of age, is already setting patterns for the shape of his or her life. These patterns of thought and practice will either serve the glory and purposes of God or hinder them.[17]

In some respects, my experience with and observations of our resident population was a gift serving as a cautionary tale. My newfound awareness pressed me to ask questions of myself. Who was it that I was becoming? Equally important, who did I not want to become? What were the characteristics in others I wanted to emulate? To what degree could I control or shape my temperament, personality, and disposition? Is it harder to establish new habits or break bad ones? After reading Fleming's book, further introspection led to questioning the "patterns of thought and practice" that existed in my life that needed to change. What ideas and practices needed cultivating? Was I serving the glory and purposes of God or hindering them?

Of some things I was sure: I knew I truly wanted to honor the Lord in my life, and I sure as heck didn't want to end up as Mrs. Crankypants who complained for the sheer sport of it. I also knew God met me right where I was and loved me just as I was (a reality that draws me back to the Lord again and again), but I also knew He was *taking* me somewhere in this faith journey, that the promise of transformation was real. I longed to bear the fruit characterized in Galatians 5:22–23: "But the fruit of the Spirit is love, joy, peace, patience, kindness, goodness, faithfulness, gentleness, and self-control." But how?

> God calls us to be so much more than becoming the best version of ourselves; He calls us to conform to the image of His Son.

For starters, God showed me that He calls us to be so much more than becoming the best version of ourselves; He calls us to conform to the image of His Son, to be transformed into *His* likeness.

> We all, with unveiled faces, are looking as in a mirror at the glory of the Lord and are being transformed into the same image from glory to glory; this is from the Lord who is the Spirit. (2 Cor. 3:18)

> For those he foreknew he also predestined to be conformed to the image of his Son, so that he would be the firstborn among many brothers and sisters. (Rom. 8:29)

> But our citizenship is in heaven, and we eagerly wait for a Savior from there, the Lord Jesus Christ. He will transform

the body of our humble condition into the likeness of his glorious body, by the power that enables him to subject everything to himself. (Phil. 3:20–21)

I had a choice: I could become more of what I already was by my own willpower, or I could become more like Him through the power of His Spirit.

I may not fully understand what it means to be conformed to the image of Christ, but I do know it is a supernatural work of the Holy Spirit, transforming me from the inside out. Romans 12:2 tells us, "Do not be conformed to this age, but be transformed by the renewing of your mind, so that you may discern what is the good, pleasing, and perfect will of God." Similarly, Ephesians 4:23–24 piggy-backs that verse: "To be renewed in the spirit of your minds, and to put on the new self, the one created according to God's likeness in righteousness and purity of the truth." Taking these together, I'm persuaded what my mind consumes—books, entertainment choices, online content, the company I keep—influences and shapes my spiritual formation and character development.

God gives us absolutely everything we need to grow in our knowledge of and love for Him in order to become more like Him—His Word, His Spirit, His people, and more. But these are like any other precious gifts we receive. We have to take it, open it, and use the gift as it's intended. Otherwise, how can it make a difference?

You, like me, have the choice to become more like what you already are, or to become more like Christ. And if you want the latter, you have to behold Him in order to become like Him. This isn't to diminish your personality, your giftings, or all the little quirks and idiosyncrasies that make you you; God created you as unique, and He meant to. But, if it's true that we become what we behold, it is vital to be intentional and careful about what (or Whom) we're beholding.

Left to our own devices, we might drift unaware, never dying to ourselves and leaving little room for transformation. Or, we could look around at others and try to become like them, losing sight that God created each one of us for a special purpose that brings glory to Him and blessing to our world. If we focus on hurts or grievances or life's disappointments, a root of bitterness could grow deep and we could end up a Mrs. Crankypants.

My retirement community years proved to be a classroom in life and also in faith. Among a wealth of "caught lessons," one valuable piece of advice I learned is this: to set patterns of thought and establish practices that are for your good and God's glory, *right now*, by focusing on Jesus. You're under the influence of whatever you've set your sights on, so if your eyes begin wandering—looking to others, culture, or even within yourself—you've already taken your eyes off Jesus and that will create problems down the road. If your patterns of thought and practice have you darting your eyes in any other direction it's critical to re-focus. Only when it's Jesus you're beholding will you find yourself looking more like Him. And that takes practice.

11

BEHIND THE CURTAIN

Pay no attention to the man behind the curtain!
—L. Frank Baum, *The Wonderful Wizard of Oz*

When I was pregnant with our first child, I worked out a neat, little arrangement with my boss at the retirement community to return to work on a part-time basis. Following my two-month maternity leave, we agreed that I would spend two–three days a week in the office, averaging ten days a month. It was ideal, a win-win proposition for both of us.

I wasn't the woman who had always dreamed of staying at home with her kids; quite the opposite, actually. My aspiration was to be a "professional business woman," though who knows what I thought that meant as a twenty-something. My role as a marketing director for a mid-size continuing care retirement community wasn't exactly globe-trotting or glamorous, but it was meaningful, manageable, and more than just a job to me. I genuinely loved the people I rubbed shoulders with every day.

My back-to-work plan was the perfect arrangement. Well, it was until Rachel, at five weeks old, began smiling—not just reflexively, but on purpose, in response to cues from Tad and me. Who can resist a gummy infant grin? I was toast.

Tad was more than glad to see me smitten with the little creature we spawned. While I might not have had my sights set on being a stay-at-home mom, that's how he had grown up and what he had preferred all along. The part-time arrangement I had negotiated with my boss had been a compromise. With no family in town, we investigated alternatives for childcare, but good options were hard to find. None seemed to be just right. This, and Rachel's precious, toothless smile nixed my interest in returning to Westminster Towers.

I met with my boss to let her know about my change of heart and intention once I was sure I wouldn't change my mind again. Thankfully, her response was gracious, and she opened a door for me to work in an occasional consultant role instead. Our conversation couldn't have had a more favorable outcome.

Being Rachel's mommy 24/7 was magical. Until it wasn't. I didn't mind the constant demands of caring for a newborn. It wasn't that I was tired, either. Rachel gave me the incredible gift of sleeping through the night at four weeks (you'll hate me more to know Thomas did this at one week. I know, I know . . . a miracle.). It was a combination of things I hadn't anticipated—lack of adult conversation, isolation, deprivation of intellectual stimulation, four walls closing in.

On top of those things, there was the lack of getting paid. I hadn't realized that my paycheck wasn't only about contributing to our budget; it also assigned value to me. I felt worthless at times even though my head (and Tad) told me I was doing the most important job on the planet, and that "paychecks" would come in other ways (i.e., I'd never miss a "first"—rollover, word, step . . .).

Inevitably, a wave of guilt would crash over me for not being thankful enough that Tad and I were able to make it work financially, or that I had a husband willing to make sacrifices so I could be home. I knew others who longed to be in my shoes but had to go back to work to make ends meet. What was wrong with me? I adored my baby girl and loved being with her, so why wasn't I content? Feelings in conflict with one another ignited a vicious cycle of self-loathing. Mom guilt has a million ways of rearing its ugly head, whether you work, stay at home, or do both.

A few weeks after I had officially resigned from my job, a friend with an older daughter stopped by to drop off a meal and gift and to meet Rachel. When she asked how I was doing, I sensed she was interested in an answer beyond "fine," so I took a risk and told her the truth: I was struggling and having a hard time reconciling my feelings and discontent.

"You have to *learn* to be at home," she said matter of factly. She had my attention immediately. She had an explanation. "You went to school a lot of years in order to get an education so you could get a job. Your entire life trajectory up until giving birth was about working. You prepared for that, but maybe you never prepared for this."

Ohmyeverlovingword . . . What a light bulb moment! Carol's insight helped decode my feelings and lift the grip of guilt. What may have come more naturally for other moms wasn't so natural for me, but that didn't mean I was awful or broken. Her words gave me the freedom to give myself a break and to recognize what I was doing was new to me. I had to *learn* this thing. What a relief.

This conversation with Carol was a pivotal and poignant memory because it's the very moment I realized how critical it was and is to have women in my life who have gone before me. Advice from others even just a few years ahead of me, in age or stage of life or spiritually, is invaluable. Carol's wisdom and encouragement opened my eyes to see what I had missed.

As the weeks and months marched on, I adjusted to life at home. I learned how to master timing so I could shower, go to the bathroom, brush my teeth, grocery shop, cook dinner, do laundry, and maybe even eat ALL IN ONE DAY. My sense of accomplishment was redefined.

We marveled at our little girl. You get new eyes when you have a baby, don't you? It's like you finally, *finally*, see the wide-eyed wonder of life. Sometimes I was so overtaken by the miracle of her, I wanted to grab complete strangers, shake them silly, and scream, "CAN'T YOU

SEE THE MIRACLE?!" I had taken so much for granted, and through our daughter, the Lord flung open doors of revelation.

Still, I struggled at times with my value and self-worth. I believed I had made the right decision, I was thankful to be home with her, but I missed my job, and the validation, stimulation, socialization, and pay-check that came with it.

Nine months after Rachel was born, opportunity came knocking: the nursery director at our church decided to step down, and she asked me if I was interested in her position. Initially, I saw it as an answer to the unspoken prayer of my heart—a meaningful, part-time job, and not just a job, but ministry (imagine doe eyes and floaty hearts circling my head). The time commitment was minimal, based on eight to ten hours per week. I'd be managing a combination of paid staff and volunteers on Sunday mornings and evenings, Wednesday evenings, and special events. The pay wasn't great, but this was ministry (right?), and I wasn't only considering it for the money. With the exception of our Tuesday morning staff meetings, I could keep Rachel with me or let her stay in the nursery when I was handling calls and administrative details.

After discussing the pros and cons, Tad and I decided this sounded like a good fit for our family. I interviewed with our Director of Christian Education, received an offer, and started work right away. I was excited to feel like I might make a difference for the families I'd be serving, and thankful this job allowed me to stay home with Rachel or at least be with her most of the time.

That I was also the only person interested in interviewing for the position should have been telling. The honeymoon ended the next week. The entire paid staff announced they wouldn't be returning on Sunday mornings when fall programming started up only a few weeks later. I was thankful they at least agreed to work our evening nurseries and special events. I had gotten to know these ladies as a mama prior to stepping into the nursery director role, and I knew they loved our babies well. The continuity they offered on Sunday mornings would be a loss.

Their departure ushered in significant changes to the way we'd staff our nurseries going forward. Rather than replacing these ladies with a new paid staff, I was directed to transition our care to all volunteers. Our church was large (more than a thousand members), and there were lots of babies. Surely, everyone would agree with my philosophy—if you use the nursery, you'll willingly and happily take a turn to serve, and if your children are older or out of the house, you'd selflessly offer your time to give weary mamas and daddies a break.

Bless my heart. Wasn't I precious to think such a thing?

Mostly, the transition from a paid staff to all volunteers went well. Yes, there was a lot of educating and re-educating about the changes in practice and philosophy, but many folks stepped forward to commit to service. Still, I was naive, ill-prepared, and over-accommodating. Focusing on getting both of our Sunday morning worship services covered, I created levels of service in order to provide church members options: one month per quarter (four months per year), one Sunday per month (twelve Sundays per year), and even lesser options. Honestly, the bar was set pretty low, but the pushback had been considerable. No one was willing to commit to a year of service. It may not have been pretty or efficient, but it was a way to get it done.

Everyone assigned for service received a copy of the master schedule including member phone numbers. Theoretically, the onus was on the volunteer to switch dates with someone else on the list if they had a conflict. (There I go being precious again.) More often than not, they called me to take care of it. I'd usually begin those calls by deflecting the responsibility back to the caller, but sometimes it was just easier to handle it myself. The distinct ring of an old school landline makes me twitchy to this day.

Our church was either drinking water from a prolific fountain or taking seriously God's command in Genesis 1:28 to "be fruitful, multiply, fill the earth . . ." In other words, lots of babies were being born. Before I came on board, church leaders had given the go-ahead to build a new nursery wing to accommodate growth, completed soon after I joined our staff. It was a humongous improvement over our previous cramped space, bright and beautiful with plenty of room for the under-twos to jet around. In fact, there was so much space begging to be used, the next year we decided to offer a weekday parents morning out program (PMO). Though I didn't know a thing about early childhood education, I had good sense, a nearby Christian bookstore with plenty of materials, and a toddler who was adept at schooling me in anything else I needed to know. Remember, this was pre-Pinterest and pre-anything on the internet that provided ideas and inspiration. Google wouldn't be invented until four years later. Bless.

Church leadership gave me considerable freedom in creating our program. As long as tuition covered our variable costs, they were hands off, trusting me to handle the details. The church assumed our fixed costs.

I loved this new challenge. It allowed me to use my experience in marketing, communications, sales, and PR in a new way. Essentially, I was responsible for running all aspects of a small business.

I developed a two-year, rotating curriculum. I designed and provided copy for a brochure and registration forms. I wrote an employee manual and trained our staff. I promoted our program within and without our church, and met with parents as needed. I set up a budget, handled tuition, published a monthly newsletter, and resourced our classroom with supplies. I'm sure there were a few hiccups along the way, but overall it was satisfying. I felt a strong sense of accomplishment from its success.

I was in an unusual position because I was hired for one job but created a second when we launched our parents' morning out program.

I was savvy enough to build in compensation for myself for managing PMO, but, again, because the program was self-sustaining, dollars were limited. I also wanted to make sure our staff earned a decent wage—they were the rock stars of our program because they were the ones in the trenches with our babies and toddlers.

Everything seemed to be going well save one thing: No one seemed to notice when the hours I worked doubled . . . and then tripled . . . and then quadrupled. Even I didn't notice at first. But I suspect anyone who works in a part-time position at a church eventually learns there's really no such thing as part-time.

In my case, from the get-go, the hours allocated for the nursery director job were underestimated because of the impact of the paid staff's departure. The transition to all-volunteer Sunday morning staffing translated to more time.

Talk to any nursery director of a large church and they'll tell you it's one of the hardest jobs on the planet. You're dealing with mama and daddy bears who are fiercely protective of their babies (and rightly so). Most church folks are reasonable and understanding. They appreciate the volunteers and staff who care for their little ones. It's the one or two unhappy campers who make you earn your stripes the hard way. I remember the day our college pastor's wife called to check on me after church because she had noticed tears streaming down my face the entire service; one of the usually soft-spoken mothers whose child was in the nursery that day had read me the riot act over how I had handled something. She was completely unreasonable to me and downright mean, and it was one of those times it's best to keep your mouth shut. I walked into the worship service a wreck, my body betraying my emotions. I was still a pleaser in this season, and I took criticism related to my job too personally.

For the most part, I loved my job, well, jobs. I favored the one I had more control over—the PMO program—but both provided a sense of accomplishment and making a difference in people's lives; not just our parents, but even our volunteer and paid staffs, and those darling babies entrusted to our care.

It's interesting, but you can really tell who has a heart for God by the way they serve others; by contrast, it's evident who serves out of a sense of obligation or duty. In my role as church nursery director, I could write a proverb about it—

> "A joyful countenance reveals the heart of those who delight in serving God, but the one who begrudges his work cannot hide a bitter spirit."

And all the nursery teachers said *amen*.

It was also beautiful to watch volunteers and staff thrive in their roles, taking ownership of their territories, and tossing blessing around like confetti. They took initiative and didn't wait on me for direction—this was strong evidence of a commitment to excellence in their service. It is in these places that I began to notice the subtle difference between serving and loving God by loving and serving others versus serving and loving others to serve and love God. There's something to God being at the center of why we do what we do as opposed to Him simply being a recipient of our best effort.

As nursery director, one of my responsibilities was also attending weekly staff meetings. At first I was intimidated by this circle of pastors and staff, but soon enough I realized mine was a privileged position. I learned about the inner workings of our church, I got to play a part in planning and programing, I was a voice and advocate for children and their families, and more than anything, I learned how to pray. Just listening to incredible men and women of faith pray taught me so much, and they inspired and encouraged me more than they'll ever know. And it wasn't that their prayers were fancy or overly intellectual—I still remember Tim, our youth pastor at the time praying, ". . . and Lord, convict the snot out of us . . ." God is surely reserving a special place in heaven for youth pastors, Young Life leaders and their ilk (holla, Craig and John!). But as funny as it was to me, it showed me an intimacy with the Lord I didn't realize was possible. Talking to Him like a friend—that was allowed?

Thomas was born less than two years after Rachel, and I was back at work within two weeks because a) I could keep him by my side, and b) the kid's first gift to me was sleeping well. I didn't have the good sense to take more time off—I felt a responsibility to my position and the people I served—and no one told me to take more time off. Somehow I managed to juggle those two babies and the ever-increasing demands of my job and hardly miss a beat.

For four years I worked both jobs, clocking time for a full-time job and getting paid for part-time hours. My personality and work ethic didn't allow me to work "X" number of hours and be done with it; I'd do whatever it took to get everything done. I didn't micromanage my PMO staff, but I also didn't delegate as well as I should have. I loved and respected my boss, but he had his hands on a lot of other moving parts, and I don't think he realized the weight of all I carried. I needed an advocate.

I couldn't see it when it was going on, what working those two jobs was doing to my life spiritually. Nor did I understand how damaging it was for me to learn about the underbelly of our church—that in some ways it was a business and a political arena where deals were made and agendas were advanced depending on your social currency. At least that's what it looked like from where I sat. I never quite reconciled how the wealthiest men in our church also happened to be the godliest, as evidenced by those who sat on our elder board.

It was a great church in most regards, where people had shepherded and loved our family well; yet it was an imperfect institution because her people were imperfect. In my naiveté, I expected so much more, and I can see now how my lofty expectations weren't fair. I was privy to many of my church's imperfections because of my job; I had seen the "man behind the curtain," and that would bear consequence.

By the time I decided to resign my position as nursery director and only lead the PMO program, the damage was done. Cynicism and skepticism had crept in. I judged people by my measure of godliness, and that was tied largely to their visible church service. I was judgmental toward parents whose children benefited from our programs and classes, but who did not serve in ministry themselves. On the flip side, I was also critical of parents of older children, who didn't feel a call (or more accurately, a sense of responsibility) to provide some relief for those mamas and daddies with toddlers underfoot. That martyr spirit led me to make blanket assumptions about members and their willingness to serve, but I bet I was dead wrong 99 percent of the time.

> It's possible to be right in the middle of an opportunity that lines up with your gifting, your passions, and your real-life schedule, and *still* be wandering.

I couldn't tell at the time that it's possible to be right in the middle of an opportunity that lines up with your gifting, your passions, and your real-life schedule, and *still* be wandering—into places like bitterness, anger, record-keeping, cyncism, works, self-righteousness, and burnout. No doubt, my church had its sin issues that needed to be uprooted—most churches do, I suspect—but so did I. I couldn't see that I was in bondage, chained to my definition of godliness (which didn't always happen to align with Scripture). Worse, when others didn't meet my expectation for service, essentially becoming enslaved the same way I was, I became frustrated and judgmental. I was juggling way too much, feeling like I needed to do it all, but I expected *you* to do it all too. I was oblivious to the speck of wood—or let's be honest, the redwood forest—that had taken root in my eyes.

My nursery season was so complicated as it seeped into my faith. Suddenly seeing the church I loved as a *business* along with the junk (sin) attached to it was disillusioning. I felt like Dorothy in *The Wizard of Oz* when Toto pulled back the curtain, and what I saw left me unsettled and disoriented.

It would be a while, but eventually God would pull back the curtain of sin in my own heart, and that would prove painful as He loved me enough to make it personal.

People wander, and as it turns out, churches can be wandering, too, just in different ways. The good news is that God never wanders. He always, *always* remains faithful to you, to me, and to His bride, the church.

12

SURPRISE PARTY

Nothing weighs on us so heavily as a secret.[18]
—Jean de La Fontaine, *Fables*

Resigning as our church's nursery director was a healthy decision for me, both spiritually and emotionally. Though I continued working with Parents Morning Out, my role wasn't considered core staff, and that provided a safe distance from the business side of the church. I loved our little program and the teachers and families we served, and the time commitment was much more manageable. That mattered even more by the time I gave birth to Stephen, our third child in less than five years. This darling little boy didn't value sleep like his older brother and sister. If I ever imagined that Rachel and Thomas sleeping through the night was a result of me being a great mom, Stephen set the record straight. I had nothing to do with it.

Life clicked along. Raising and wrangling babies, making time for me and Tad, maintaining our home, and working and serving at church kept me busy. The days lasted forever but the years whizzed by. How could Stephen be old enough for kindergarten?

Five years earlier, I couldn't have imagined ever wanting to move. My job had become fun again and I wasn't so stressed at church. Our roots burrowed deep and our boughs stretched wide. Life was good, too good, maybe, and we were happy and comfortable and clueless about what was to come.

There had been an opportunity to move not long after Stephen was born, but I'm not sure we even gave it serious consideration. Just visiting the town where the job was had given me the doldrums. I wasn't budging.

Looking back, it's almost laughable how I dug my heels in, how tightly I held on to a place. I was an obstinate fool to think we were in control.

God didn't pry my clenched fists open all at once. He took His time, loosening one stubborn finger after another.

For a while Tad's company had been drifting away from its folksy roots; the family-oriented corporate culture he had joined ten years earlier was no longer recognizable. About a year after we decided not to follow that job lead, a seismic shift rattled the ground beneath me. In the playlist of my life, I refer to that moment as "the day the music died . . ." Though it sounds melodramatic, I sensed immediately it was only a matter of time until Tad left his job, and *that* felt huge. The event itself was rather small and ordinary, like in the way a tiny pebble can crack your windshield if it comes at you with enough force.

On this particular day the tiny pebble coming for us was when Tad's boss reversed a decision he had made; a reversal blamed on budgetary concerns but one Tad felt like could cost them more in the long run. Had the atmosphere of the company been what it once was, it would have been another day at the office. Instead, this amounted to the proverbial straw breaking a camel's back. Between this decision, the change in company culture, and growing frustrations in general, I felt like Tad's days there were numbered (although I'm not sure he did).

Almost one year later to the day, he resigned, knowing it was time to move on. As he transitioned out, he was careful not to burn the bridges he had been building for years; he valued the relationships he had with so many good people. We trusted that the Lord was leading him toward something new and different, and the changes at his work had merely been the catalyst.

For the next three years he owned his own business. For the first time since we had children, he could take the kids to school, and he had freedom to attend field trips and programs he might otherwise have had to miss due to work. We didn't necessarily view his business as a forever solution, but in the short-term, it was the right thing for our family.

Meanwhile, we were in that season where your children's activities dictate how you spend your time. Beyond church and work, community was birthed in the bleachers of an indoor pool, along the sidelines of a soccer field, in a crowded, noisy gym. I had changed the diapers of most of my kids' friends and knew their parents long before they were twinklings in anyone's eyes. Small-town living meant there was a fair amount of overlap, but since it's all we knew, that was our normal.

There's a lovely rhythm to life when you've been in a place a while. It's a bit sad to think that so often we don't appreciate it or know it exists until it's gone. Such familiarity is like your favorite cozy sweater, yummy comfort food, a fuzzy pair of slippers—something you enjoy but probably take for granted.

Do you remember the tale of a frog in the pot? If you drop him in boiling water, he'll jump right out, but put him in lukewarm water and slowly increase the heat, and he won't realize the danger he's in until it's too late. When we had been presented with that possible out-of-town job opportunity all those years ago, it was dropping us in an already-boiling pot. I jumped out before I was even good and wet. But not long after we returned home from our fact-finding trip, our hometown "pot of water" began to heat up. It started when one of the couples closest to us moved away . . . then another . . . and eventually another.

Bizarre things started happening. A series of hateful and extremely hurtful anonymous letters were sent to a few people in Agape, still our Adult Bible Fellowship (ABF). Based on the letters' contents, it became obvious that the note was from someone within the class, and the collateral damage went well beyond those who received a letter. Not long after this, some of our closest friends never seemed to have time for us anymore, basically ghosting us before I had ever heard of such a thing. There was no fight or falling out, just a gradual dwindling of affection I couldn't seem to overcome. I had a huge misunderstanding with yet another friend, and though I think we both tried to find our way back to each other, our relationship was never quite the same.

Around the same time as these largely personal losses, our church changed the format of our worship services. Originally, they offered two blended services on Sunday mornings that incorporated elements of both traditional and contemporary worship styles. The new format created a distinct service for each; members would now choose a service based on their style preference for worship.

Because the services took place at different times, it effectually forced a split in our beloved ABF as member preferences were divided. In the aftermath of the anonymous letter debacle, these worship service changes were the second in a one-two punch, inflicting a mortal wound from which the class would never recover. Our class dissolved soon after.

We had been invested in the people of our class, closely attached on a spiritual and emotional level. When you're a member of a large church, you need a smaller community to be known and loved so you can, in turn, know and love others. If you've ever been a member of a larger congregation, you know what I mean when I say our class was like a little church within the church. Even though at times feelings had been hurt or there were misunderstandings, we were still a family who loved one another.

The deconstruction of our class affected members in different ways. For us, the loss was deeply personal, probably more so for Tad as the lead teacher. Once we lost that class as an anchor, we were adrift in a big ocean, wandering but at least together in it. It was so odd and sad to feel like strangers in a place that once felt like family.

But what's the big deal about a few friends moving out of town, a few more moving on, and a Sunday school class disbanding? What's the harm in an anonymous letter or a church deciding to change up its worship services? In a word, *relationships*. Each of my losses were relational, whether collectively or individually. It wasn't that I had been holding onto a place with a white-knuckled grip; I was holding onto *people*. We didn't live near family, so friends became our most significant relationships beyond our children and each other. These were the people with whom we were doing life. We knew each other well—birthdays, anniversaries, handwriting, for goodness sakes—all those small nuances of a person impossible to fast-track. It's one thing to find a kindred, an instant "What? You, too?"[19] connection, and another to build a friendship in the trenches, where you've logged time, grown up together, served one another across a table or shoulder to shoulder, and wiped the noses and bottoms of each others' babies.

Several years and a series of conflicts and losses brought me to the point where I was not only willing to move, I *wanted* to. Tad, having accomplished several important work-related goals, seemed to be in a place of completion with his business, maybe even a little antsy. As an engineer he's a great decision maker and problem solver, and he missed the challenges that go hand-in-hand with a complex production process.

It was about this time his former employer called to gauge his interest for a position that would move us out of state. He had visited the site once before, and back then he had mentioned how beautiful the area was and that he wouldn't mind working there one day. (Of course, at the time he said it, I wasn't having any of it. Funny, the difference a few years and a change of circumstances made.) The more he learned about the new job, the better it sounded, and I was finding myself increasingly ready for a new adventure.

But if I've learned this once, I've learned it a thousand times—life is rarely an "all or nothing" proposition. I still loved our hometown and her people. It was the place all my babies were born and the only place they knew. Tad and I had been growing roots there for almost our entire marriage; just because I was a little battered and bruised didn't mean I could leave and never look back. Though our community wasn't as cohesive as it once was, we still cherished those with whom we had spent the last fifteen years doing life together. Even the friendships that had struggled in recent years mattered to us.

This is the spot I found myself as my fortieth birthday approached. Though Tad and I knew he was going to accept the job offer in Tennessee, we hadn't told our children yet; his parents and my sister were the only people who knew. We planned to keep the cat in the bag for a few more weeks until more of the details were finalized.

Celebrating birthdays is one of my favorite things to do, whether yours or mine; they're a present in and of themselves because—*h e l l o !*— another year of life! Of course, children love birthdays because of the gift potential, but I think I especially value them because the "next" one isn't guaranteed. Making it to my fortieth birthday meant I had already lived two years longer than my mother. While some people dread their fortieth, I viewed it as crossing a threshold into a really special club. Age is its key to entry, a luxury not afforded to all.

My sister, Lora, had asked me if I wanted to plan something special, but the weekend of my birthday we were headed out of town. The children couldn't have been happier since that meant a trip to Noni's and Grandy's farm. Since we weren't leaving until Tad got off of work, I was thrilled when three sweet neighborhood friends invited me to lunch at a favorite restaurant. The Garden Cafe in tiny York, South Carolina, makes a life-changing buttermilk pie, and if you're ever lucky enough to make it there with only time for a meal or dessert, I suggest the latter.

I was so preoccupied with our secret about moving—and conflicted because I wanted to tell my girlfriends what was going on in our lives— it never occurred to me to suspect they had something else planned besides lunch. I didn't put two and two together when the host directed us upstairs though there were plenty of tables available on the first level. Not until I reached the top stair, rounded the corner, and was smacked in the face with a raucous "Surprise!" did I begin to process that I just walked into a party for me . . .

Stunned, I found my place at the head of a long banquet table, encircled by women I love. Most of them would never have suspected the depth of my years-long struggles, my sense of loss, pain, or void. None of them knew that I felt like I was floating in that ocean of uncertainty about the future, wandering and wondering in my heart of hearts. Like I said, life is rarely an all-or-nothing proposition, and despite my angst, there was still a lot of beauty I could point to—these women and their friendships being first in line.

Overwhelmed by this incredible show of love, tears filled my eyes as I crossed my arms on the table and buried my face. I was the only person in the room who actually knew what was going on.

No one else could have possibly known this wasn't a birthday party at all. It was a going-away party. In three hours I'd be on the road bound for Tennessee for a weekend of house-hunting.

Technically speaking, I suppose it was a surprise party, but as time would reveal, the surprise was on them.

13

THE MAGIC OF
STARTING OVER

*I have always been delighted at the prospect of a new
day, a fresh try, one more start, with perhaps a bit of
magic waiting somewhere behind the morning.*[20]
—J. B. Priestly, *Reader's Digest*

Moving and starting over at forty sounded like a great big, exciting adventure to me, poetic even. A milestone event for a milestone birthday. It's natural to romanticize new beginnings, I think. An optimist holds that blank slate with reverence and expectation, eager to begin writing—living—all the wonderful things to come. Beginnings are when skies are the perfect cast of blue. Beginnings hold endless possibility.

Telling our children about the move had gone about as well as something like that could: it ignited a snotfest in the middle of our den. It is the only time I can remember the five of us clinging to one another for dear life. This alone makes it a precious thing to me, a binding of family through the solidarity of tears. Believing this was the best choice for our family didn't mean it was easy, though.

Tad and I showered our babies with assurances, but I suspect we needed to hear those words as much as they did. We gave them freedom to grieve leaving the only place they had known as home, but keeping in mind we were the grown-ups, we framed the move to help them to see it in a positive light.

Sensing the Lord's leading in all this fueled my excitement. I had witnessed my own 180-degree change of heart relative to moving. Whereas a few years earlier I wouldn't consider such a thing, now I was practically begging for it. It may have been circumstances loosening my grip, but I couldn't see it apart from God's sovereignty, some great cosmic gift to bless us and answer prayers the way I hoped.

(That makes me laugh hysterically now.)

I landed in Chattanooga with my arms open wide, eager to begin our new lives. The house we bought was our first two-story, a blue Victorian giant perched atop a hill. Ironically, I had preferred any color other than blue for a house—I had loathed but lived with the blue trim on our previous house for years—but it checked the rest of our boxes and met the children's sole requirement: to be near a creek. A dribble of a stream had bounded our house in South Carolina, and it had been a favorite play spot of theirs. Being the American mom I am, my dream house included a comfortable master bedroom and bathroom, a roomy kitchen, and plenty of space for company, but being the American kids they are, all they wanted was a decent watering hole. That we found such a house surely was a sign we were on the right path.

The first weekend in our new house, we took a break from the unpacking to go on a family adventure. Ever since spotting an overgrown path at the back corner of our yard, we were eager to discover where it led. All five of us braved a thick tangle of brush and bramble, carefully navigating the downward, sometimes slippery slope and sidestepping snares of poison ivy. Our efforts earned a reward beyond anyone's expectation: the path plopped us right at the bank of Wolftever Creek. Wide and winding and breathtakingly beautiful, this was a ten thousandfold upgrade from the pitiful little trickle we once revered.

The kids splashed in and out of water as we headed south along the creek's edge while our hike kept getting better and better. First, we stumbled upon an old rope swing dangling from a branch fifteen feet above the water. Weathered slats, nailed into the tree's trunk ages ago, served as a rickety ladder. Reluctantly but always a mom first, I ventured into the water to make sure it was deep enough to handle a jump—fully clothed, mind you, because this wasn't on the agenda when we left the house. For kids ten, nine, and six, this was as good as it gets. They were all so brave to me, monkeys scaling a tree and swinging loose and wild. Every childhood should be built on such things.

From there we walked a little farther and came upon what we imagined to be some sort of Eagle Scout project, an intricately-constructed rope bridge suspended across the creek. To all appearances it was long-abandoned; fortunately for us, it was still intact. We all tried our hand at it to dubious success. It reminded me of a carnival rope ladder game, the one that flops you off right when you think you've got the giant teddy bear won.

A bit farther beyond the rope bridge, we made yet a third discovery—caves! We didn't venture very far into their tunnels—it would be years before my children became spelunkers—but we were thrilled to find so many natural wonders in our backyard. If I had a top ten list of Best Days of My Life, this one would make the cut. It was the stuff of a magical beginning.

We filled our days getting to know our new hometown and even welcomed a few out-of-town guests to our new place. We bought a membership to the local aquarium and visited so often we were on a first-name basis with the fish.

Still, there was a somber loneliness to our days. There's a weightiness that companions not knowing anyone where you live. Even if we were still in South Carolina and had gone a long time without seeing anyone outside our family, it would have felt lighter knowing friends were within playing (or hugging) distance. Thankfully, we enjoyed the company of each other, but I knew our kids missed their friends. We were all eager for school to start so they could begin making new ones.

Getting pictures on the walls and moving boxes out of sight made our house feel homier and settled our spirits. With a bonus Nature's Playground (the creek) skipping distance from our backdoor, home was quickly becoming my first Happy Place in Tennessee.

Tad and I had already decided I wouldn't get a job since Rachel, Thomas, and Stephen were still in elementary school. We knew once sports and activities kicked in, I'd be donning a chauffeur's hat.

At the time we were strong advocates for Christian education, and we found a school that shared our philosophy for a covenant-based approach; it was the most similar school we could find to the one we left behind. In contrast to a missional or evangelistic model which would allow students from any religious background (or none) to attend with the hope of them hearing the gospel and eventually coming to faith, a covenantal school requires at least one parent to profess belief in Christ, and to be in agreement with school policies and core beliefs. Older children typically have to share a personal testimony of faith.

On the first day of school I scribbled my name on every classroom volunteer sheet you can imagine. I agreed to tally lunch count, stuff weekly homework folders, serve as a co-room mom, paint walls, and drive every carpool. With three kids in grade school, opportunities to help were endless. I didn't mind, though; I had nowhere else I needed to be. Teachers and administrators must love new families who come in with so much energy and so few competing commitments; ask anything of us and we'll probably say yes.

The children shared a common campus, but their grades met in three separate buildings. Rachel and Thomas envied their baby brother. Stephen had hit the jackpot with his classroom; first and second grades were located in a brand-new building finished just in time for the start of school.

In an attempt to preserve their shiny linoleum floors, teachers asked students to bring in tennis balls cut with one-inch slits to slip over desk and chair legs. The morning of the due date to send in Stephen's tennis balls, I remembered we hadn't yet made incisions in each. I didn't want to ruin good kitchen knives or blacklist my kid for failing to meet a deadline (he had reminded me, but Mommy was a slacker), so I dug out the Leatherman tool from the glove compartment of my car. While the children ate their cereal and got ready for school, I started hacking.

Have you ever tried to puncture a tennis ball with a Leatherman tool during the early-morning, before-school hustle? I don't recommend it. In case you're wondering, it's not as easy, as say, slicing a tomato, or even a spaghetti squash. Number one, a tennis ball is round. That means it will roll. Number two, a tennis ball is thick rubber coated in fuzz. They're made to withstand constant beating and children playing with scissors. This is what makes them an ideal "fix" for first grade desks and chairs. Number three, a Leatherman tool is great for many things but performing surgery on a tennis ball? Not so much.

Of course, none of that deterred me. I am a mother and WE MAKE DO WITH WHAT WE HAVE.

I was on the third ball when my luck ran out. As I started to hammer the tip of the Leatherman blade into the top of the tennis ball, it rolled, and I stabbed my pinky finger instead. *Hard*. It's important to note I don't do well with blood—praise God for all things pure and holy, my kids spared me from much of that. I wrapped my free fist around my finger to apply pressure, walked around the counter to the sink, turned on the water, and let it flow over my cut so I "couldn't" see it. Which should've been the end of it, except the room started spinning, and I felt like I was going to vomit. I grabbed some paper towels, wrapped them tightly around my little finger, and turned away from the faucet with the water still flowing, to face the center of the room. Slowly, I slipped to the floor, my back scraping against the kitchen cabinets, intuitively realizing I was about to pass out and trying to control my fall. I remember not wanting to traumatize my children for the rest of their lives, wondering, *Can you actually die from a cut on your pinky?!* and then I passed out.

Seconds later, I opened my eyes to find Rachel crouched next to me and Stephen in front of me asking, "Mom, are you okay? Are you OKAY??" The same Casting Crowns song was playing on the radio, the water still spewed from the faucet, but Thomas had disappeared. (I never knew if it was because he was oblivious to the scene being played out in our kitchen, or if he freaked out from his mama's fainting spell.)

I convinced them I was fine, although to be honest, it was unnerving. This was the first time I had ever fainted, and all it had taken was a tiny cut on my pinky?! I replaced the paper towels as they became saturated with blood and cut the rest of the tennis balls, slowly and much more carefully this time. Once we made it to school, I stopped by the nurse's office and she butterflied my finger. It continued bleeding for a few days, so I probably should have gone to the ER for a stitch or two, but seeing that I didn't even know where a hospital was yet, AND IT WAS JUST MY PINKY, I couldn't be bothered. Thankfully, I lived to tell.

Despite a bloody beginning, Grace Academy was my second Happy Place in Chattanooga. Next to home, I spent more time there than anywhere else. Teachers, staff, and other parents were friendly, and I knew I had to keep putting myself out there to make more meaningful connections.

My third Happy Place in those first few months was the mall. Not because of the shopping, either. It was there I was surrounded by people, *friendly* people, helping me to feel a little less alone in the world. Never have I been invited to visit strangers' churches more often than at Hamilton Place Mall in Chattanooga, Tennessee. It was borderline weird it happened so often, and I wondered what vibe I was giving off that encouraged so many invitations. No doubt Southerners are a friendly lot, but we don't necessarily mean it literally when we invite you to "stop by sometime." Or maybe I just looked like a wayward soul in need of saving, and church-minded folks were doing their Christian duty. Who's to know? While I never took anyone up on their offer, I appreciated every one.

There were more Happy Places I'd soon come to love—Coolidge Park, Northshore, Southside, Lookout Mountain and Fairyland, the Tennessee Riverpark. The Tennessee Valley is a natural beauty with enough local flavor to charm you into staying a while.

Upon discovering some wonderful new Happy Places, we also started looking for a church home (though without the help of my imaginary mall friends). Mixed emotions about uprooting our children lingered. Though they seemed to be adapting just fine, we felt all the parental guilt over forcing them to start over and endure the rabble that goes with it. We felt like we "owed" it to them to get settled into church as soon as possible. Doing so would be in everyone's best interest.

Before leaving South Carolina, a couple who had just moved to the area offered up some wise advice when they learned we were moving: *Don't look for a duplicate of the church you're leaving. You'll only find disappointment . . . start fresh and don't try to pick up where you left off.* Maybe we would have come to that conclusion on our own, maybe not, but I sensed they were sharing this out of their personal experience. We would be wise to heed their counsel.

It occurred to me that visiting a new church is a lot like going on a first date. You can gather a lot of information online first, to determine if you want to move on to the second step—meeting in person. You hope what you learned and liked from their website is consistent with what you find in person, and that you'll find a perfect match sooner rather than later.

We immediately ruled out churches too far from our house. We had lived less than two miles from our church in South Carolina, and as involved as we planned to be, we wanted to be relatively close. Though we knew of a few churches by reputation or from our former pastor's suggestions, they were location-prohibitive and we refused to give them a second thought. We also knew we didn't want to attend the church associated with the kids' school; we had done that in South Carolina, and we had learned it would be better for us not to put all of our relational eggs in one basket.

So, for an hour or two on Sunday mornings for as long as it would take, we were prepared to attend service after service and then compare notes to determine if this church might be "the one." The music, style of worship, atmosphere, the way they prayed, even the décor, could make a difference. The way we were greeted. The type of bulletin. Diversity of members and leadership. But the determining factor most of us are likely to judge more than anything else is the teaching—and the primary way to gauge that when you are new is through listening to the pastor deliver the sermon.

As much as I wish the pulpit-experience didn't matter so much, it does. You can forgive a lot of things if the theology and preaching in a church is sound and good; conversely, if the teaching is lacking and everything else is fantastic, it's hard to stick with it. When you leave a service after your first visit, you know right away if it's a viable contender for your new church home. At some point during the ride home or to lunch, your conversation will shift to what you thought of the church, and *that* conversation will undoubtedly include your thoughts about the preacher and the sermon.

Remarkably, we found our new church home on only our second Sunday of visiting churches. Someone from Tad's work had told him about a church that had asked its members some time prior to forego buying new Easter outfits in order to raise money for a young family in their congregation. The husband had an aggressive brain tumor, and their medical bills were skyrocketing. When we learned the church had raised several hundred thousand dollars, we thought it must be an indication something special was going on there.

Before the end of the service we knew we were done searching. Between the theology, sermon, atmosphere of worship, and congregational commitment to one another as evidenced by their generosity, we felt at home. Tad and I were raw in those early weeks post-move, and though neither of us are typically cry-ers, there was more than one occasion we left with wet lashes. The messages were personal and timely, exactly what we needed to hear. Church wasn't exactly one of my happy places yet, but I was optimistic; the worship service was balm to my weary heart.

We were off to such a nice start. The children adjusted to their new school and seemed to be finding their way. They had always been relatively easy kids, but their resiliency was a surprise that ministered such grace to us. Tad's job was familiar yet challenging. I had already collected half a dozen happy places and I was confident there were more to discover.

We had earnestly sought the Lord's leading prior to leaving South Carolina, sensing it was time for a fresh start. When Tad was approached about this job in Tennessee it seemed to be God's provision and plan for our family, an answer to those prayers. We trusted what seemed to be the Lord's leading, and starting over found me in a season of wide-eyed wonder, expectation, and great optimism—to me, the essence of magic.

But I had forgotten to remember an important thing about magic: it's not real. It's a short-lived illusion. It begins with wide-eyed wonder, but when it's gone, you're left blurry-eyed and wandering, trying to find where in the world it all went.

14

BACK AND FORTH

*We should be unafraid to doubt. There is no
believing without some doubting . . .*[21]
—Justin Holcomb interview with Barnabas Piper

Any magic of a new beginning faded as our new realities settled in. Moving still required hard work and intention long after the boxes were unpacked and pictures were hung. We had found our church with such relative ease I guess I was naïve enough to think assimilating would be just as easy.

When we began visiting churches in Chattanooga, as advised, we guarded against trying to duplicate our former church experience in South Carolina—or at least we attempted as much. We tried our best to hold our preferences and biases loosely, praying, seeking God, and following the sage wisdom of "In essentials unity, in non-essentials liberty, in all things charity."[22] I had always said denomination didn't matter to me as long as the church was doctrinally sound and biblically based (There are no denominations in heaven, right?); here was my opportunity to live this out.

As it turned out, the church we chose *was* a different denomination from the one we had previously attended, and it didn't take long for me to discover that my idealistic philosophy wasn't translating into real life. I am no church scholar and I may not know all the subtleties and distinctions among denominations, but I *am* a life-long churchgoer and

I'm aware of stereotypes. There were liberties to which I was accustomed at our former church that I strongly suspected wouldn't have been acceptible in our new one. Was this a matter of me projecting my perceptions or something more? No matter the answer, I wasn't sure I'd ever be able to let these people see the "real" me because, if they did, surely I'd be turned around and marched straight out the door. Though the teaching itself was sound, the social norms and freedoms differed from what I was used to. I felt like a very square peg in a perfectly round halo.

In their defense, no one in our church made me feel that way. It was solely based on my perception based on denomination. But perception is our reality, and according to my reality, I was a giant Sinner McSinnerson. Every denomination, or church for that matter, is different in its practices and sometimes in the interpretation of Scripture, and it was taking me time to adjust mentally to the changes.

As we continued to attend the worship service Sunday after Sunday, the Lord ministered to us through our new pastor week after week. We appreciated John's expository preaching style as he went deep into the Word communicating the truth we were so desperate to hear. It was all so personal, as if Jesus Himself cared enough to speak directly to us through this pastor's handling of God's Word.

What a gift.

Though we weren't quite ready to join, we went through a new member class and made a few personal connections. We also began attending an adult Sunday school class, but this was the extent of us "plugging in." We knew we needed to rest a while and to get to know our new church better before becoming more involved.

Though I didn't realize it at first, I arrived in Chattanooga carrying baggage from my previous church life and experience. Between working at the church we were members of, our children attending the church-sponsored school, and serving in various ministries, I was church-weary. We may not have been there every time the church doors were open, but it was close.

Have you been there? If you have, you already know when you're busy about the business of church you'll eventually burn out unless you're being wholly led, empowered, and filled by the Spirit. It's such a subtle thing—serving people without the primary intention of serving God. All that pouring out will deplete a soul if you aren't being continually filled by the only One who gives life. Completing a Bible study, attending a worship service, or listening to Christian music doesn't have the power to accomplish a thing. Doing religious things is never a substitute for genuine relationship with Christ, for knowing Him, spending time with Him, loving Him. As my dear friend Prancy says, "God made us human BE-ings, not human DO-ings," and that sends me straight to Psalm 46:10, "Be still, and know that I am God" (ESV). If we're running around doing all the things for all the wrong reasons, making no time for deep interaction with the Lord, how will we ever be still enough to "know that he is God"?

> Doing religious things is never a substitute for genuine relationship with Christ.

Even though we needed time to be refreshed and refilled, I felt guilty for not immediately offering up my work and service to the new church. I was buying, at least temporarily, the notion that serving was the defining mark of a true believer; not to earn salvation or find favor with God, but because my actions are an evidence of the Spirit's life in me, my obedience to God's Word, or a demonstration of what it looked like to love others. Isn't that what James 2 is all about? Well, yes . . . and no. Sabbath and rest are biblical, but my point here is that I was wrestling; with who God is, who I am in light of who He is, and what impact that should have on my life.

The irony was not lost on me that in my season of rest, I had become the very kind of person I had criticized when I served as nursery director back in South Carolina. I was tired and a little shell-shocked in this new denomination, and in no time I had become the type of member I had disdained, taking advantage of the church's programs without doing my part to support them. Funny, what a little perspective will do for you. Because I was so busy mentally judging other people back then, I hadn't taken time to understand their circumstances and find out why they weren't serving. Maybe *they* had been tired and shell-shocked for any number of legitimate reasons. Maybe they had needed my help, prayers, or kindness more than I needed their service.

Though our pastor's sermons ministered to us so personally in those first few months, I found something troubling among some of the people I was meeting. There seemed to be a pattern of playing favorites with certain leaders in our church community, a practice cautioned in James 2:1–9: "My brothers and sisters, do not show favoritism as you hold on to the faith in our glorious Lord Jesus Christ. . . ." Adult Sunday school classes weren't lauded for their sound teaching or community but because of the leader who taught them; and when I asked questions about a particular class, I often received a glowing endorsement for the teacher. I also detected a collective sense of pride about the church itself that went well beyond really liking your local congregation. Members were quick to let me know that several well-known authors and speakers attended our church, as if their pedigree elevated the church's value. There was a subtle air of superiority, as if these famed or renowned people should impress me. (Had I been acquainted with these notable leaders, I might've bought into it, but because they were new to me, I was unimpressed.) The former pastor who left years earlier was so dearly beloved, church members continued to speak of him with such reverential awe and lavish praise I imagined he might just walk on water. While enjoying your teachers, appreciating your leaders, and loving your former pastor aren't at all sinful, something didn't feel right about how ordinary people were so highly esteemed. Instead of making much about God, it was more typical to hear something great about the church or the previous pastor or certain teachers. Jesus was lost in a crowd on a pedestal.

I had never observed anything like it, this esteeming of particular leaders and teachers, and it rubbed me the wrong way; was that arrogance I was sensing when members spoke of our church or my imagination? The Scripture that invariably came to mind when this happened was Proverbs 16:18— "Pride comes before destruction, and an arrogant spirit before a fall."

I genuinely wrestled with what I was seeing; was this a matter of me being discerning or plain old judgment rearing its ugly head? Maybe I was making a mountain out of a molehill, and perhaps my observations weren't a real problem. Maybe this was me sitting on a high horse, or somehow related to being a fish out of water in my new denomination. This was a difficult season, after all, and maybe my vision was clouded.

Though we had been very active in our church in South Carolina, Tad and I had been slower to engage in Tennessee because we needed to recover from burnout. Rested and ready when a new adult Sunday school class was formed, we decided to offer our help. The leaders of the class were as new as us, but I noticed how well they already seemed to be regarded among church staffers compared to us. They had come to our church from another large church within the denomination, one of those mega-churches with a well-known senior pastor under whom they were discipled. They let us know they had everything under control for launching a new Sunday school class, a tried-and-true model for success. There was a smugness to it all that didn't sit well with me. But on the flip side, what if God was showing me what my own tight-knit community from our old church had felt like to newcomers?

So, now I wasn't just Sinner McSinnerson, I was also Judger McJudgerson. I knew what Jesus said about judging people, and as I pointed a finger at others I noticed the three aimed back at me. I wondered about the beams in my eyes I was too blind to see. This couple leading our class loved Jesus and wanted to use their knowledge and experience to disciple other believers. I had wanted to lay low for a while, fly under the radar, and take a break from church service, and yet it bothered me for a strong couple to lead out? I wanted to have my cake and eat it, too, and my conflicting feelings were at odds. Humans are complicated, aren't they? Rather than celebrate the giftings in two people willing to serve, I found fault. What in the world was going on?

I think, looking back, I was experiencing a twofold battle—one, between Satan and myself, and two, between my flesh and the Spirit. The enemy was tempting me to judge my new church family, condemn them, or feel shamed by them, creating a relational divide between us before we even got to know one another. As for my internal battle, in Spirit-led moments, I knew I really did need to rest for a season and that others taking the wheel of leadership was a good thing. Also when led by the Spirit, it was understandable for me to be at odds with glorification of people over God. The Christian celebrity culture is real (and wrong), and although what I observed in our church was on a much smaller scale, it had the same feel. And yet, if I'm completely honest, in fleshly moments, there were times I wanted to be known and highly esteemed myself (we had a taste of that in our former church and maybe I missed it).

I sure didn't want to be wandering, feeling disconnected from the body and distant from God. Church had become so complicated.

Never once did it occur to me that it could have served my church well had I been brave enough to share my concerns with someone in leadership. That maybe, just maybe, our church would have benefited from a course correction, or at least hearing out one of its members, and evaluating whether there was anything (sin) to address.

It is one thing to be an habitual complainer or a Nellie Naysayer, finding fault with everything, especially when it comes to matters of preference. But it is an entirely different animal if you're concerned about a practice or ethos that dishonors Jesus in any way. I felt like I was the only one who had a problem with or even saw the collective pride in our church body (I would find out later I wasn't). But even if I was the only one, if I was following the Lord's leading, a loving conversation would have been a great place to start.

What if I had mustered the courage to talk to those few church members and leaders about how they were coming across (dismissive and haughty)? I was *for* them, I genuinely cared about them—we were church family! I have no doubt these people loved Jesus but what I witnessed was damaging to their testimony and credibility.

Why are we often quick to dismiss our opinions, to assume we've got it all wrong, or to believe we're right but do nothing? Where is the love in that? Why do we perceive our church leaders don't want to hear member concerns? I suppose some send that message but other times we're likely making wrong assumptions. Or is it a matter of fear? Who stands to gain when we remain silent, if indeed, there's blatant, unchecked sin?

It's vital to seek the Lord, earnestly and with a pure heart, in order to distinguish sin from our own pettiness, preferences, or insecurities. But I'm convinced if you lead with love, have a winsome and humble spirit, and your goal is unity and God's glory, it's worth an uncomfortable moment or two to get things out in the open and make them right. Being for and loving one another makes the difference.

Because I was struggling in life and questioning my faith, I second-guessed myself to pieces. Consequently, I diminished the value and soundness of my opinions. What the Spirit was revealing to me was right, but because the flesh was also raging, I kept my mouth shut.

I didn't consider it at the time, but all this back and forth I felt in my heart was really just the age-old, basic Christian's battle between flesh and Spirit. Not to mention Satan is always against a spirit of unity among the body of Christ. All this season-to-season fighting for faith when I didn't feel like it, wondering what in the world was wrong with me, and wrestling with holy and hard things was actually pretty normal for most people.

Years later, it would come as a lovely surprise to realize sometimes wandering can be just a different sort of season of walking with God.

Years later, it would come as a lovely surprise to realize sometimes wandering can be just a different sort of season of walking with God.

15

ONCE UPON A BLOG

People are slaves to whatever has mastered them.
—2 Peter 2:19 (NIV)

Wrestling, for me, is largely a head game. It can happen when I overthink my circumstances, make comparisons between my ideals and realities (what I want versus what I have), and when I take my eyes off Jesus. The struggle between our flesh and the Spirit is real.

Over two years into our lives in Tennessee I still felt like a newcomer. On more than one occasion I found myself revisiting a conversation Tad and I had before we moved from South Carolina.

"When all is said and done, what if we never find community like this again?" he had asked.

Right in the middle of packing up all our earthly belongings and pioneering west, Tad had raised a question I didn't want to hear. Ever the realist, he wasn't second-guessing our decision to move as much as he was acknowledging the relationships we were leaving behind.

His question had come on the heels of a big going away party hosted by a group of sweet friends. Almost everyone we had come to know over fourteen years showed up to bid us farewell. Each conversation was a gift as friend after friend shared how Tad or I (or both of us) had impacted them, some recounting stories we had long since forgotten; not because they weren't of value to us but because after fourteen years, sometimes you need a little help remembering.

Our moving prompted people to tell us things we might not otherwise ever have learned, and it was both beautiful and overwhelming. I can only hope we returned a portion of what we received that day as their recollections stirred our own fond memories.

My love language is "words of affirmation"[23] so it's understandable how such an event would overflow my love-tank, but even Tad was visibly moved by the kindness and generosity extended to us. I remember feeling like I was the wealthiest person on the planet. When all is said and done, I agree with the Proverbs when they say our greatest treasures have little to do with silver or gold.

Leaving on such a high note naturally made us wonder if one day we might regret making a good career move at the expense of leaving a special, hard-won community. It hadn't been without its flaws, but that's never the point anyway, is it? It was dependable and loving, a life-well from which we drank and were refreshed.

It probably would've helped us detach more quickly had our last days in South Carolina not been so good.

I had arrived in Chattanooga with high hopes and great expectations. Within a short amount of time I had collected a handful of happy places. The children were making friends and doing well in school. Tad's job had its challenges, but overall it was promising. Yet two years into our move, life was not turning out like I had hoped. I was homesick for something I couldn't quite put my finger on, and my best approximation was a place. The community we had before may not have been perfect, but I would have packed up and retreated to South Carolina in a skinny minute.

As it was, I returned to visit as often as I could the first few years after our move; sometimes with Tad, sometimes as a family, and a few times on my own. I longed to be with people who knew us well and with whom we shared history.

Tad and I learned quickly that our approaches to South Carolina visits were vastly different, a source of contention at times. He was content to hunker down with the friends with whom we were staying, and I wanted to bebop all over town seeing as many people as possible. Having worked at my church for ten years and carrying great affection for our staff, if we were there during office hours, I'd try to see my former coworkers. I'd squeeze in some hugs for the residents at the retirement community I worked at, too, since it was right behind the church. And then I'd scramble all over town from one friend's house to another, racing against an invisible but very real clock that cruelly sped up time. It was energizing and yet exhausting, and I always felt like I was disappointing someone—either my visits were too brief, I couldn't get to everyone I hoped to, or when we had more than one offer to stay with someone, feeling like we were hurting someone's feelings. Tad's way was probably the better way, but I'm wired to overcommit and I couldn't seem to help myself. I'd scurry and hurry and pay a price every time.

After those visits I'd come back to Tennessee filled with a dread I couldn't seem to displace. Though I was usually the one who spots silver linings in the darkest of clouds, a gloominess lingered in my head and heart. We lived in a beautiful part of the country. Our children were thriving. Why couldn't I fully embrace where we were? Why was it so hard to be content?

Some of the answers we *could* identify were tied to the decisions we had made two years earlier, even before we moved. While our choices made sense to us based on what we knew at the time, without realizing it, we had put ourselves at a disadvantage. I imagine most of us make decisions much the same way. We pray and sift through the information relevant to the opportunity at hand, evaluate the possible options, and make a thoughtful, deliberate choice, hoping and praying all the while that, on the other side, we will see that it really was the best decision possible. We do the best we can with what we know.

As I've alluded to, we faced three major decisions with our move to Tennessee, the type every family encounters when relocating: where we would live, where our children would attend school, and where we would go to church.

We chose a house in a neighborhood centered between Tad's new job and the children's new school.

We chose a school about fifteen minutes from our house because it bore the closest resemblance to the school our children had previously attended.

We chose a church, also about fifteen minutes from home, because it checked all the boxes for our "essentials."

Each decision was made after carefully and prayerfully weighing our options. On the surface, every choice appeared to make perfect sense and meet the needs most important to us. But as time would eventually tell, those choices bore unforeseen consequences. Every choice in life does this, I suppose, bringing positive or negative results you couldn't have anticipated. In our case, the consequences to our decisions made life challenging. For instance, one of the reasons we bought our house was because of its large lot; I liked the idea of living in a neighborhood but Tad valued the privacy our almost three acres provided. Win-win. Perched atop a hill at the end of a long, winding drive, our house sat well off the road. But living so far off the street at the end of a cul-de-sac meant it took longer than normal to get to know our neighbors. If we noticed someone out walking, even if we bellowed a "hello" at the top of our lungs, the closest resident would've had a hard time hearing us. And it never crossed our mind that once our children started driving they would have to travel an incredibly busy and potentially dangerous stretch of interstate to go virtually anywhere. Several major trucking companies headquartered in our area only exacerbated the issue. Their number, size, and speed made them potential killing machines in my mama-eyes.

Soon enough, we would also come to understand both the children's school and our church had a regional draw. The practical implication meant new friends could live as far as an hour away, problematic when you're trying to arrange a kid's playdate or have company over for dinner; someone was going to have drive a ways. We were more than willing to do the heavy lifting in order to foster relationships, but it certainly made everything harder.

Being part of a community was one of our highest values, and unwittingly, we had set ourselves up for that to be an uphill battle. Relationships weren't developing naturally and easily the way we had experienced in our past. Our children weren't going to school with neighborhood kids. The people we were meeting at church often lived far enough away that getting together was a hassle.

These were obstacles that could be overcome, no doubt. But it made life difficult in a way we hadn't anticipated. I was volunteering at the school as often as possible, I attended church and area Bible studies, and though I had managed to make a few friends, the community I idealized and longed for continued to be elusive.

It was so odd—we "knew" how to nurture relationships, or based on the fruit we saw in our previous efforts, I think we did. We were initiators, eager to invite people into our home, but invitations were seldom reciprocated in our new hometown. Friendships remained surface-y and polite. Every time I felt like I was finally going deeper with someone, momentum stalled. Was this a stage-of-life thing, a cultural phenomenon, or was something else going on? Was I subconsciously keeping others at arm's length? Was I expecting too much too soon? It was bewildering.

I suppose in some ways I was trying to duplicate what we had had in the glory days of living in South Carolina, against the advice we had been given by that new couple at our old church. We had been cautious enough not to do that with our place of worship, per se, but my image and ideal of community was what we had experienced while living there. There was a sense of doing life together that we couldn't re-create in Tennessee—in or outside of church.

I wrestled with being lonely and unhappy, but if you met me you probably wouldn't have known. I kept it masked behind a smile. It was hard not to look at the good things in my life and wonder why I just couldn't suck it up and get over myself. I thought surely things would turn around soon . . .

And then I received an email that changed my life.

It was hardly that dramatic, though. There were no trumpets heralding the moment and announcing what was to come. But I suspect the trajectory of our lives is often altered that way, by small events and ordinary moments we fail to recognize as significant until hindsight tells us so.

> The trajectory of our lives is often altered by small events and ordinary moments we fail to recognize as significant until hindsight tells us so.

All it took was a friend asking me to read something she had written.

I had known Jen through our church in South Carolina and we loved her to pieces. Perfectly suited as a youth intern, she was smart and warm and had a depth beyond her years. On occasion, she babysat for us, and after we moved, she and I stayed in touch.

Her email included a link to her blog. I had entertained the idea of creating a "weblog" as they were known in the Dark Ages, after reading an article in *Parade* magazine earlier that year; but I didn't fully understand what a personal blog looked like until reading Jen's. That's hard to imagine now in our overly social-sharing culture, but back then blogging was still becoming a thing. (To my darling Gen-Xers and Millennials—this was when your parents still had a landline and your only computer was a centrally-located desktop.) I clicked her link and read the attached post . . . and then another and another and another. I probably read everything she had written before finally closing out my browser and deciding it was time to figure out how to create one of those blog thingies for myself.

I'm a verbal processor—I suspect many writers are—and I liked the give and take I found in publishing content online. Put your thoughts out there and potentially connect with others across the country, or even around the world. We take it for granted now, but in those early days of blogging the novelty was appealing.

Not long after reading that first blog post from Jen, I launched my own blog. From my first post on, I wrote as if I had an audience, though no one had a link to my site for six months; and then, only a trusted few. I was a timid turtle with my head tucked deep inside my shell when I started writing online. *S l o w l y* I ventured out by commenting on other blogs. When those bloggers began returning the favor, commenting to one or several of my posts, I was hooked. The whole process was such a different animal in the beginning, sweet and largely reciprocal. Readership grew organically. When I read another blogger's post I'd also likely read its comment thread, and if I liked a particular comment, I'd follow the commenter back to their blog. This is how we'd find new writers to read.

At the time, Facebook was mostly confined to the college set, and Twitter was a fledgling infant. The best way to find new blogs to read was by following links to other bloggers and by engaging in comment sections. We were so much more cautious then; it's rather darling compared to now. For years my profile picture was my feet at the beach. We didn't blog under our real names and we certainly didn't share pictures of our children. We wondered if the people on the other end of the computer were actually who they said they were, or instead, deranged serial killers.

What began as sporadic postings eventually became daily routine. My reading and commenting community grew.

Now, looking back, I'm mortified at some of my blogging practices. If I discovered a blog and liked it, I would go back and read every blog post, commenting along the way. I wish I were kidding. It wasn't like there was a ton of content since blogging was newish, but still . . . I didn't fully understand how this might be interpreted (weird, predatory, or pathetic), I simply wanted to get to know the bloggers I was reading better. It was incredibly flattering to me if anyone took time to go back and read my earlier posts, especially since I was invisible-by-design the first six months I wrote online.

When I started blogging, I had no long-term plans, or short-term goals for that matter. It never occurred to me to carve out a niche. I wasn't trying to accomplish a thing. I simply had the time, I enjoyed writing, and it seemed like a fun creative outlet. I had determined I didn't want to identify as a "Christian blogger" writing exclusively about faith, but I certainly didn't have any intention of hiding it, either. Faith is the filter through which I process life, and it would naturally find its way into my writing.

I never expected to make friends, but eventually I got to know the people in my reading circle fairly well. We participated in the same blog link-ups and carnivals (where everyone posts on the same topic and links to a master list), and we had entire conversations in comment threads; relics today. If a blogger commented to one of my posts, I always visited their site, read at least a post or two, and thoughtfully commented to their writing to return the favor. I did my best to respond to every comment on my blog. It was common courtesy, good blogging etiquette, and Golden Rule living as far as I was concerned. The way things were in the baby years of blogging was rather sweet.

As more people began reading my blog, I was adding more blogs to my own reading list. My "hobby" was taking more and more time to manage.

For about two years this was my practice, writing blog posts and reading and commenting to other blogs. I had no idea what that looked like to friends back home. (I would hear a little about that years later and it hurt my heart.) And whereas I couldn't seem to find community where I lived, I became more and more attached to my blogging community.

I cannot tell you exactly when things shifted, but one day, overnight, blogging changed. It happened in a collective sense, but it also changed for me personally.

In the collective sense, brands began to notice the influence bloggers had with their readers. For starters, a good word from a prominent blogger could translate into new customers, increased brand awareness, and sales. They looked for ways to vet and connect with bloggers, and there was no better way than to sponsor a blog conference. As conferences popped up all over the country, bloggers flocked, eager to meet their online friends in real life, to learn more about their craft, and hopefully, to connect with a brand and secure opportunities to work together.

Suddenly, blogging provided a possibility for at-home moms to make a little money (or a lot) doing what they enjoyed and were already doing. To have the chance for meaningful work around the schedule of home and family was a dream. Work and compensation varied—sponsored posts, free products, trips, complimentary events, ad networks, affiliate sales, brand ambassadors, and so on. There was a lot of excitement as momentum began to build, but like anything, I suppose, there was an icky side.

Chum was in the water and the sharks were hungry. Among some bloggers, there was a palpable sense of fear there wasn't enough to go around. It made things crazy; a scarcity mentality can bring out the worst in people. FOMO (fear of missing out) was birthed in the blogosphere long before Facebook or Instagram began torturing tweens and teens.

For me, the shift came in 2008, close to five years after we moved to Tennessee. It was the year I decided to start "taking my writing seriously," which meant I was willing to invest money to learn more. I forked out what felt like an outrageous amount of money to attend a conference that helped speakers, writers, and leaders hone their craft and expand their skill set. The draw for me was a session by three well-established bloggers. I was actually nervous when we met face to face during a meet and greet, but my fears were instantly diffused when one of them recognized me, too. It wasn't that I feared being a stranger to them, but they were *Conference Speakers* and I let that comparison thing establish a hierarchy in my own head—never healthy or helpful.

It was during an audience Q&A when a simple question was asked of the bloggers that I began to feel uneasy. "How much time do you spend blogging?" Their answers, a fraction of the time I spent blogging, brought my first prick of conviction that maybe I was giving it too much time.

Another significant event happened in 2008: Compassion International, a child-advocacy ministry that pairs generous donors with those who are living in poverty,[24] hosted its first Compassion Bloggers trip. With the hope to secure monthly child sponsorships, Compassion International arranged for a group of bloggers to travel to a country where Compassion had a presence, tour the field offices, meet staff and volunteers serving in the local projects, and visit homes and families who had a child sponsored through Compassion. The idea was for these bloggers to raise awareness about Compassion's ministry and to connect readers to children awaiting sponsorship. Already vetted as wonderful storytellers, the bloggers painted a beautiful and at times harsh portrait of their daily experience, and my own heart was shredded. Coming face to face with unimaginable conditions and egregious poverty, all I wanted to do was help.

Suddenly I had a blogging goal. What better way to use your voice and influence than to speak on behalf of those who have no voice? Could my words actually be a key to "releasing children from poverty in Jesus' name"?[25] Every conscious decision I made about blogging after that initial trip was to grow my readership in order to earn the right to be asked to join a Compassion Bloggers trip. From a stewardship perspective, I understood that numbers and reader engagement mattered. This wasn't a popularity contest for popularity's sake; it was about having a reach and influence large enough to help the most children and their families possible.

My personality lends itself to networking, and because I read and commented to so many blogs, I made a lot of connections. This was my natural bent long before blogging was on my radar, but it certainly became more valuable as I set my sights on being chosen for a trip.

I worked hard to connect with people online, and I delighted in meaningful engagement. Doors began opening. Eventually through my connections, I was given the opportunity to establish and manage the faith channel for *Blissfully Domestic*, a now defunct online magazine best known for Blissdom Conference for bloggers. I was thrilled to speak on panels at Blissdom, and later, Type-A blogging conferences, but mostly to meet people in real life I had known online for years. The (in)courage brand from DaySpring, an online community for women, invited me to join the original writing team for the site—before we even fully understood what a collaborative site could be. I worked with regional and national brands, and my in-box was full of pitches and opportunities. Other bloggers frequently asked to bend my ear.

Every day was a hustle. I was writing most days, and my readership was growing. It wasn't huge, but my commenting community was engaged and I had consistent visitors. I linked up to big blog carnivals in order to boost my numbers, usually by offering some sort of a giveaway. When it came to working with a brand, I only accepted offers from companies that made sense to me. It was important for partnerships to feel authentic and honest, but I could justify about anything if it involved storytelling.

Among my real-life friends it became an on-going joke that "anything you say or do might be blogged about you." I would never have embarrassed anyone, but real people make great blog fodder. Sometimes it seemed like people were actually disappointed if I didn't write about something we experienced together, though that was not the case for my family. I had to learn the hard way that not all of my children (or Tad) appreciated posts that drew attention to them.

My blog was gaining momentum in February 2009 when another blog conference rolled around. I could barely contain myself when I learned I was likely being vetted for a Compassion Bloggers trip.

One night during the conference, I was standing in the doorway between mine and the adjoining room, chatting with a few friends. I vividly recall something I confided to them: "I feel like I'm standing on the edge of a precipice . . ." My blog readership had been trending upward, and I felt like it was about to take off.

Weeks after the conference, I would get that call inviting me to join the Compassion Bloggers on a trip to Kolkata, India, later that spring. All my hard work and grand intentions were paying off.

I'll say this: I was consistent. Just like when I launched my blog, I still wasn't writing exclusively about faith. My faith had found its way into my writing here and there, but increasingly, I found myself struggling and wandering when it came to deep and abiding belief. I wasn't focusing on bringing glory to God or relying on Him or even seeking Him in my writing because I didn't have to. I was self-reliant, I knew my strengths, and I played to them. I was striving to achieve. Though I did have a good and genuine desire for my words to impact the children and families represented in Compassion International, I had tasted a tiny drop of worldly success, and I wanted more. Without meaning to, I was making much of myself, or at least trying to.

Wandering can begin anywhere.

Wandering can begin anywhere—in a church, in seasons where life is good, or even when you're pursuing a goal. Which is essentially what was happening with me as a writer. Ever so subtly, my blog and all the things that came with it had become an idol and a source of pride. Based on the amount of time, thought, and resources I devoted to it, blogging had become too important. Had you pointed this out to me I probably would have been defensive and disagreed with you, but how I spent my time was telling.

Anything can become an idol—your spouse, children, job, hobby, health, a relationship, fitness, appearance, shopping, your education, home, perfectionism, prosperity, a job title, your phone, social media engagement—yes, even good things can become idols when they demand too much of your attention. I winced when I read 2 Peter 2:19 in the NIV version—"people are slaves to whatever has mastered them." Only God is worthy of our worship, and when we displace Him to worship something else, it damages our relationship with Him and robs us of the freedom we're intended to have in Christ.

> Even good things can become idols when they demand too much of your attention.

Blogging in and of itself isn't a sin, but I had allowed it a place of preeminence in my life, and *that* was a grievous sin. It had become too important to me.

When I was at that conference in 2009, telling a room full of friends that I felt like I was on a precipice, I was all smiles, imagining my trajectory to continue upward, headed toward some measure of worldly success that would suggest I had finally made it. The opportunities coming my way were surely an indication, right?

> Only God is worthy of our worship, and when we displace Him to worship something else, it damages our relationship with Him and robs us of the freedom we're intended to have in Christ.

It didn't occur to me when you're standing on a precipice there are actually two ways to go. God, in His infinite kindness, allowed me to tumble down.

16

EMPTY

Is it not a curious thing that whenever
God means to make a man great,
He always first breaks him in pieces?[26]
—C. H. Spurgeon

One of the things that prompted our eventual decision to join our church in Tennessee was the strength and effectiveness of the pastor's preaching. A gifted communicator and expository teacher, John taught in a way that brought Scripture to life, encouraging and challenging us week after week. His love for Jesus was contagious and his humility appealing.

When you're fortunate enough to have a strong pastor, it's easy to put him on a pedestal, in a position to be worshipped. If that happens, it is dreadfully dangerous. Not just for him, as your church leader, but also for you, as a believer. To fight this tendency, it's helpful to recognize that pastors are sinners just like you and me. By remembering they are imperfect, fallible creatures with their own personal struggles, it helps to maintain perspective. The last thing they need is to receive glory from man. Any Jesus-loving preacher would agree that robbing God of his glory is a bad idea. Yes, we should respect our pastors and be thankful for their service, but we should guard against taking their words as gospel or letting them slip into a place reserved for God alone. When pastors end up on pedestals, they have the potential to gain too much power and lose accountability. News headlines tell too many stories of those who've fallen from high places, leaving in their devastating wake a sea of broken and bewildered hearts.

I can't say if I put John on a pedestal—I sincerely hope not—but I know he was the main reason we kept coming back and eventually wanted to join the church. God used his sermons to minister to us so personally. I truly believe the Holy Spirit, who was already aware of our circumstances and needs at the time, enabled him to speak directly to our hearts and minds through God's Word. What a generous, God-given gift during a time when we desperately needed it.

When John had come to the church four years before we arrived, he had to fill the giant shoes of the highly revered pastor who preceded him, under whose service the church had seen tremendous growth. I only knew the former pastor by reputation—it was above reproach—but it was evident he loved Jesus and served Him well. I would've liked to have known him.

This rich-historied church we found ourselves in had a long and beautiful legacy of men and women who sought and served Jesus. And yet, still, there was a check in my spirit when I heard long-term members speak of their former pastor or current leaders with effusive praise. I continued to dismiss it, irritated at my own critical spirit, and sometimes even found myself telling others about the Christian powerhouses who attended our church—doing the very thing I disdained. The heated battle within me of flesh versus Spirit never seemed to die down.

During the same season I was seeing an uptick with my blog, momentum seemed to be opening new doors for our church to live out its Kingdom calling. Our numbers were growing and there was a large building plan in our future on a nearby piece of property; consequently, our church building and site were up for sale. Our leadership anticipated even more growth when we moved to our new location, and to help prepare to care for new members, they established new adult Bible fellowships. Tad and I were among a few couples asked to lead one, and we couldn't have been more thrilled for the opportunity to serve in this capacity again. We had enjoyed our support role with our previous class, but we were excited to jump into leadership once more.

Plans were progressing smoothly for the church . . . until a wrinkle appeared.

One Sunday morning our pastor announced he'd be leaving, sensing the Lord calling him to a new congregation in his home state. What may have come as a surprise to us certainly wasn't a surprise to God, but that didn't mean we were without disappointment. We believed a church should never be about a man, but selfishly, we were sad to lose someone who impacted us so deeply spiritually.

Early on in the process to find a new pastor, our church leadership reached out to the pastor who preceded John, the one with whom so many long-time members seemed to be enamored, to gauge his interest in returning. He declined. I wasn't privy to all the behind-the-scenes information available to our search committee, but it was bothersome to me to pursue the church's former pastor. It felt like an attempt to recapture the past, and it seemed, well . . . unhealthy . . . to go after someone who had left to follow God's leading elsewhere. Feeding into my ongoing perception and concern about church pride, it felt like this man was too highly esteemed for anyone's good.

Our current building sold somewhere around the time of John's departure, and we knew we'd have to find another place to meet by the following spring when the new owner took occupancy. Though our church owned additional property and had a long-term building plan, constructing a space that could accommodate our needs in such a short period of time seemed impossible. We didn't have a senior pastor, finances were tapped, banks weren't lending . . . and the clock was ticking. Circumstances looked dire.

Some folks say what happened next was a miracle.

Instead of trying to complete the entire building project on the new property, a plan was formulated to build a smaller portion of the project, multi-use facilities that would accommodate corporate worship, classrooms, and offices.

Enough money was raised to convince a lender to finance the rest. Construction crews worked tirelessly for months on end. And just in the nick of time with all glory to God, they got 'er done.

We worshipped in our new multi-purpose building the very weekend after we had to be out of the old. It was a new beginning in the life of our church and excitement and hope filled the air. It may have been a minimal build out, but it was sufficient to meet all our needs.

In addition to the space ready for use and fully functional, the revised plan also included constructing the exterior walls of a large sanctuary. It would remain an empty shell for the time being, but once we hired a senior pastor and recovered from moving, we would be able to start a new building campaign to finish it out. The crowning touch was a giant steeple practically touching heaven and completing the illusion of a finished structure. If you didn't know better when you turned down the long driveway, you'd think construction of the entire project was complete. It was a beautiful facade, the promise of something wonderful to come.

After the move, Tad continued teaching the adult Bible fellowship we helped launch prior to relocating, and everyone worked on strengthening the relationships within our class. We were grateful for special leaders who sowed light and life into the lives of our children, the older two in youth group by now.

And, still, we were without a senior pastor. Our church had a careful vetting process that would take time, so we were grateful the search committee provided occasional updates to share their progress. In the interim, our pulpit was a revolving door of church staff, elders, and guest preachers. By all appearances, it seemed no one from within our church would become the next senior pastor. The search crept along.

After about a year, members started leaving. What began as a slow trickle seemed to speed up as one year turned into two. Even so, Tad and I made the decision to stay put. That our children were settled was a large part of it, but we kept thinking *surely* our search committee would find the right person soon. It was a test of patience, but given their thoroughness, we were bound to end up with a wonderful pastor.

We had been shepherdless for so long I had a hard time keeping in mind that it is *God* who ordains pastors to shepherd their flocks. I'm not talking about putting a man on a pedestal, but there is place for a person who knows the overall needs of a congregation and offers direction and biblical teaching to address those needs.

I was getting increasingly frustrated. Actually, it was worse than that. I was growing to hate going to church, and I could barely tolerate Sunday mornings. Sunday school was good, but as soon as we'd reach the gym where our worship service took place, I'd get this sick feeling in the pit of my stomach and want to bolt. I'd pray through the entire service confessing my harsh spirit, and begging God to change my heart. I appreciated the men who filled our pulpit—I liked them on a personal level though I didn't know them well—but I was having an increasingly difficult time sitting under their teaching. Guilt attached to my poor attitude. I could neither confess nor bootstrap myself out of it, but their style and substance left me wanting.

There was this ongoing, inner battle I wrestled with week after week. I wanted to put myself under whoever was teaching on any given Sunday, to submit to the spiritual authority over me, but it was growing progressively difficult to do so. Not everyone who filled our pulpit was gifted when it came to preaching. It had been tolerable at first but as time went on I could not imagine how our leaders felt like this plan was in the best interest of our congregation. I suspected a number of factors were at work, including the search process itself; plus, there were plenty of rumors that only fueled speculation.

Maybe you've been in this hard place, too—should we stay under teaching that isn't great because the church is in a temporary crisis? Should we stick it out because of our commitment to this community? What if temporary isn't really temporary but rather a sign the church is headed in the wrong direction, and we need to exit? If teaching is the game-changer for any given church, at what point do we accept that what is being taught is no longer a good fit and move on?

Questions like these swirled in my mind the longer we went without a pastor. I wrestled with what we were witnessing, struggling to show up week after week and losing trust in and respect for our leadership. Were there candidates who could have met our struggling congregation's needs but were never given a chance? I didn't have the inside scoop but it was hard to believe there were so few viable candidates. It was easy to become critical of our process as the position remained unfilled.

I was becoming increasingly disillusioned with church in general, and it didn't help that I was struggling on a personal level. If it had been up to me alone, two years in limbo with no senior pastor, I would have moved on. And yet, Tad was still loyal, committed to our Bible fellowship and not wanting to uproot our kids. I valued his loyalty and followed his lead, but that didn't mean I wasn't exasperated.

Around this time a new family joined our Bible fellowship. As we got to know them, we found that Joe was a young pastor who had come to our church to learn. He had previously pastored small churches, but after meeting and being discipled by one of our elders, he sensed a church like ours could teach him much.

It didn't take long for us to discover that Joe was well acquainted with the Bible. Tad led our class by asking a lot of open-ended questions to engage as many members as possible. Joe's responses were always based in Scripture. As we got to know Joe and his wife, it was impossible not to notice his esteem of and love for the Word. His mastery and handling of Scripture made me want to know it better myself.

Church leaders were getting to know him, too, and one Sunday when all of the regular interim preachers were unavailable, he was invited to preach. I was blown away. Joe was a natural in the pulpit, and his sermon brought conviction without condemnation. I had never heard anyone like him, all the more impressive because he wasn't seminary educated or formally trained. Joe's was a Damascus Road testimony just before his twenty-first birthday, and his response had been to immerse himself in Scripture. He seemed to take seriously and literally Psalm 119:11, to hide God's Word in his heart. His spiritual knowledge and influence was genuine. It wasn't that he had all the answers, but he demonstrated incredible potential, and God's call on his life to preach was undeniable.

I'm sure if you had polled church members at the time, you would have had varied opinions about Joe; there would be plenty of people who preferred the leaders I had a difficult time listening to. I have also been around long enough to discern when church politics are at play; long-term friendships and relationships carry weight. But when Joe preached, I wasn't angry or fighting myself throughout the service. I praised God for the conviction of the Holy Spirit. When sin was revealed, I repented and thanked God for the forgiveness available to me in Christ. Joe wasn't asked to preach as often as the other regulars, but every time he did I was amazed by his ability. God was the only explanation that someone so young, new to the faith, and not formally trained or educated could communicate Truth so clearly. Joe pointed me to Jesus and made me want more of Him.

One Sunday morning there was an announcement that Joe was joining the staff as an associate pastor. It was made clear he wasn't stepping into the role of senior pastor; he had neither the experience or qualifications yet. Nevertheless, we were thrilled. By now he was a friend and we knew he was eager not just to serve God, but to learn more so he could better love and serve others.

But then things got sad and ugly.

I don't know all the details of what happened next, but from the outside looking in, this is what we witnessed:

The next Sunday morning, without a lot of explanation, it was announced Joe's offer was rescinded. We knew that not everyone shared our view of him, but the explanation we were given hardly began to justify this chain of events. As slow and meticulous as the vetting process had been all along for a senior pastor, I couldn't imagine that Joe would have been given an offer had he not been thoroughly examined. (It definitely wasn't a matter of some big secret being discovered about Joe after the previous Sunday's announcement.)

It felt pointless to approach someone in leadership to discuss what happened. As an outsider I never felt like my opinion would have been valued. At best, I may have been patronized, but more than anything, I knew nothing would change.

Not long after this, Joe was called out of our church to pastor another local congregation.

The weeks dragged on, months passed by, and after almost four and a half years without a senior pastor, we finally decided to leave. With no small measure of grief, Tad announced to our Bible fellowship he would be stepping down from teaching to enable us to visit other churches.

The next week it was announced the church's former pastor, the one who served prior to John, had accepted a call to return to the church.

Today as I'm writing, over ten years later, I'm so glad to hear good things about our former church. There's a new pastor on staff, and the church has continued to maximize use of the space it completed during the original construction for its partial build. Nevertheless, the expansive sanctuary with a towering steeple you can see from the road is still just a beautiful facade, the promise of something wonderful to come but empty inside.

Back then I didn't realize how much I had in common with that sanctuary veneer; looking whole and complete on the outside, but sometimes struggling and just as empty on the inside.

17

TUMBLING

*There was once in man a true happiness, of which
. . . now remains . . . empty. This he tries in vain to
fill with everything around him . . . [yet] this infinite abyss can be filled only with an infinite and
immutable object; in other words by God himself.*
—Blaise Pascal, Pensées VII (425)

Believing that leaving our church was the right thing to do
didn't mean it was easy for us. The aftermath created gaping
holes in my heart, begging to be filled.

As the saying goes, nature abhors a vacuum, right? While white
space and margin are essential for our lives, too often our tendency is
to fill empty spaces with something, anything, to diminish void or to
minimize our pain. If there's a lull in the conversation, we'll prattle on
endlessly about diddly and squat rather than endure an awkward silence.
Feeling blue? Binge on dark chocolate or Netflix or shopping or endlessly scroll social media—whatever primes your dopamine pump.

We can do the same thing when it comes to the voids in our lives
that relationships should be filling. I was looking for deep and meaningful connections with a small group of people in my backyard, and
when it wasn't materializing exactly as I hoped, or when it took longer
than expected, I began filling my emptiness with my blog and the

connections it provided. It wasn't a conscious decision. In fact, I'm sure at the time I didn't have a clue what I was doing.

When there's a hollow in our hearts begging to be filled, we can substitute the one thing we need—Jesus—with a million things we don't. For me it was my blog, but all of us have our thing. Work. Children. Marriage. Food. Our appearance. Fitness. Hobbies. Social media followers. TV. Politics. Sports. Shopping. Civic work or volunteerism. Friendship. Romance. Money. Even ministry or church work—whatever gives us comfort in the moment, a pacifier we can use for comfort or relief.

> When there's a hollow in our hearts begging to be filled, we can substitute the one thing we need—Jesus—with a million things we don't.

We had been in Tennessee around five years and my homesickness for South Carolina had thankfully long gone by the wayside. Now in my mid-40s, I had never been more comfortable in my own skin. And yet oddly at the same time, self doubt could creep in about all the things I hadn't accomplished. The temptation to fill the empty void with accomplishment instead of Christ was alive and well.

I had purposefully given up my career to be at home with my children, and now that they were older and didn't need me as much, I found myself excited about the opportunities beginning to emerge for bloggers. I was eager to do "something more" with it, I just wasn't yet sure what that looked like.

To develop myself and figure out what my "something more" might be, I attended writing and leadership conferences. I enjoyed working behind the scenes at the weekend blogging event hosted by Blissfully Domestic while also having the chance to network and learn from people who knew more than me. On top of this, I still had my dreams set on a future Compassion Bloggers trip. As my experience and connections grew, I felt like I was riding a wave of momentum. Remember, too, I had confided to my blogging friends that I felt like I was on a precipice, sensing my blogging/writing career was about to take off. I had high hopes. Some of those holes in my heart were beginning to fill.

Still, closer to home I was facing void on a number of levels. No area seemed immune to struggle—marriage, family, church, identity, friendship, faith. Some battles were largely exterior but others raged in the interior places—in my heart, mind, and spirit. No wonder I was clinging to my blog.

Both Tad and I were struggling individually. Tension between us had been mounting for a while, and part of that stemmed with frustration and disappointment from not finding "our people." We were lonely. He was under pressure from work that went beyond business as usual. We were both grappling to be happy on our own which made it difficult for us to be happy together. We certainly weren't following Philippians 2:3, considering each other as more important than ourselves.

I can't speak for him, but I was suffering from an inexpressible, ill-defined, internal pain and void. And without ever speaking it out loud—maybe not even realizing it—I was blaming him for not meeting my needs.

When we were finally approaching the end of this valley, we would come to suspect both of us had been dealing with some level of depression birthed in circumstances beyond our control and likely also tied to our age. But melancholy was foreign to us, a never-before spoken language we didn't recognize; we really didn't know what we didn't know. For most of our lives success had come easily. We were strong, resourceful, and self-reliant, and could handle most anything that came our way. And we had plenty of pride to get in the way of us asking for help.

Tad's love language is acts of service.[27] He loves me and our family well by working hard and providing and maintaining a beautiful home. He coached the boys' sports teams. There wasn't any home improvement or repair project he wouldn't try. He managed our finances and handled yard work and car maintenance—I can't imagine how much money he's saved us through the years.

There were times I felt unloved by Tad but the reality was I was deaf to how he was speaking it; love wasn't being communicated in my primary love language—words of affirmation.[28] It's crucial to note he *was* loving me the best way he knew how, but he was speaking it in *his* native tongue, which was indecipherable to me. I wonder how many of us are walking around on the receiving end of a love expressed in a language we don't understand, and therefore not feeling loved (even when we really are)? I wouldn't be surprised if there are many of us who are looking for affirmation and meaningful connection, who might also be missing what's right in front of them.

The by-product of having different love languages means that at the bleakest moment in our marriage when I was dying of thirst, Tad offered me a glass of sand. I likely extended the same courtesy to him when it comes to the particular ways he receives love. It is so important to remember that although Tad's love for me was falling on deaf ears, it didn't mean he loved me any less; the same is true for you in relation to the most important people in your life (spouses, of course, but also parents, siblings, and best friends). A wanderer can be blind to truth because her vision is obscured by credible lies.

> A wanderer can be blind to truth because her vision is obscured by credible lies.

My children's I-love-yous came freely and frequently, but it wasn't like they were telling me what a great mom I was. Motherhood is an incredible gift (and my greatest honor on this earth), but for a lot of years it is largely thankless. It's not that you're serving your family to be appreciated, but sometimes, it would be nice to hear their gratitude (mamas, can you relate?). No one is intentionally taking you for granted, but it's not on their radar to applaud your hard work, either. Mother's Day is all well and good—I mean, *j'adore* their handprint art projects to this day—but a Hallmark-prescribed holiday only goes so far.

I was also still grieving my father whose end of life was a cruel and heartbreaking nightmare. His body lived fourteen months longer than his mind. For years we had noticed his mental decline but his entire medical team missed the correct diagnosis of dementia with Lewy bodies. As such, on a trip to the ER he was given an antipsychotic drug—potentially life-threatening and something you never administer to a patient with LBD—which caused neuroleptic malignant syndrome. We thought we were going to lose him that day.

For over a year while his body withered small and his mind trickled away, my sister and I took turns caring for him to give his wife and twenty-four-hour caregivers a break. My brothers lent a hand in other ways.

It had been a particularly difficult season for me to help. Daddy lived over three hours away, but our children were in school and took part in various extracurriculars—daily realities for which I was the primary one responsible to oversee. I wanted to do more, but the burden fell mostly on the shoulders of my sister. In circumstances like these, I imagine it's more typical than not to have a lot of varying opinions about what to do and how to do it. Even good relationships are stressed. Following his death, tensions lingered among my three siblings, me and his wife as we worked to resolve his estate.

Interior and exterior plates were spinning so fast I was dizzy—community was hard to find, marriage was challenging, caring for and then losing Daddy was awful, expectations I put on myself for writing were hard to live up to, and the ordinary and constant little battles that come with raising kids were ongoing. Even on ordinary days life is akin to managing a circus, but when everything converges at once, it can feel like more than a person can bear. There were voids that needed filling everywhere I turned.

And all the while there was the matter of leaving our church. A tremendous amount of guilt accompanied my feelings. People I cared for and respected loved this church and served her body as laymen and leaders (some still do). As I've alluded, knowing it was finally time to leave didn't mean it was easy.

While what was going on with our church made it an easy target, the truth was my doubts about God weren't going away. My spirit thrashed in the face of questions that were no longer satisfied with Christian clichés and Sunday school answers. I was struggling with belief; not whether God is who He says He is, but whether He existed at all. This wasn't just the usual back and forth of flesh and Spirit—it was an outright attack on everything I had once believed. I wasn't just wandering around on the ship of faith. I was considering abandoning the entire vessel.

I found solace in a familiar passage of Scripture that offered me great hope as my questions swirled. It's a story found in the gospel of Mark 9:14–25 about a father who asks Jesus to heal his demon-possessed son. The father says to Jesus, "If you can do anything, have compassion on us and help us." Jesus said to him, "'If you can'? Everything is possible for the one who believes." Immediately the father of the boy cried out, "I do believe; help my unbelief!" This boy's father acknowledges the true condition of his heart, something Jesus would have already known, and Jesus' response is to heal his son, immediately and completely.

Sometimes, "Lord, I believe, help my unbelief" was the only honest prayer I could offer. I wanted to believe more than anything, but I wasn't willing to lie, at least not to myself. But who can you admit this sort of thing out loud to? When you've grown up in the church, when you're sending your children to a Christian school, when you've identified yourself as a Christian as long as you can remember, it's not a rejection that comes easily or without shame or confusion, and oddly enough, questioning your questions.

My husband, my church, my kids, my extended family, my blog, serving others—none of the things I had always used to fill the voids in my life were working. And my faith was hanging by a thread.

Given everything that was going on in life, not to mention all the junk in my head and heart, I couldn't help but wonder, *Is this what a mid-life crisis looks like?* I imagined such a thing would be more obvious—Tad buying a motorcycle or dumping me for a twenty-five-year-old trophy wife, or me suddenly taking up B.A.S.E. jumping or resculpting my body with plastic surgery—but it was much more subtle. There wasn't anything obvious you could point to. The struggle was less about some major single event and more like a million little things gnawing away.

Have you ever played Jenga? It's a game of finesse played with fifty-four rectangular blocks, each nearly identical and three times as long as they are wide, stacked in a tower three blocks deep and eighteen rows tall. Players take turns extracting one block from the lower levels and carefully returning it to the top of the stack. Each play adds height and instability to the existing structure as gaps are created below. This point in life for me was a lot like Jenga, and maybe right now, it is for you too. At one point you're stable and sure, but over time circumstances change and holes are created—success is elusive, dreams aren't becoming reality, we're hurt by people we love, we're hurt by people we don't even like, expectations are unmet, our hearts are battered, age-related issues surface, we're sandwiched between the demands and needs of our parents *and* our children, mountains emerge, and valleys drag on. All the little blocks change places and reshape our lives, but in a way that makes us wobbly and less sure. The more our voids add up, the more compromised we are. We're sometimes only one block away from tumbling.

On the surface, when it came to marriage and parenting and church, I was fine. Because life wasn't completely horrible, I dismissed too much of what was going on as unimportant or trivial. But underneath, everything wasn't okay, and I didn't quite know how to deal with my voids, my doubts, and my questions. I mostly plowed ahead, not resolving a thing. Attempting to control one of the few things I could, I continued investing more and more time with my blog. Though unintentional, I was essentially filling the places reserved for God with sloppy seconds.

Bless my heart. I didn't have a clue what was coming next.

I was beside myself when I received an invitation to join the third Compassion Bloggers trip to India. While I had done everything I knew to do to position myself as a viable candidate, it was still the best sort of surprise to receive the call. Compared to many, my blog audience was small. I understood that it didn't matter how hard I had worked; it still needed to make sense from a sound stewardship perspective for me to go. I believe the tipping point for me was my connections. My reach was amplified because a few bloggers with larger audiences were willing to let me guest post on their sites during the trip.

To speak on behalf of those who have no voice is always an honor and privilege, and I was eager to do everything within my power to help secure sponsorships for children. In addition to meeting the child I sponsored, I couldn't wait to meet our team in person. From what I could tell, it was a fantastic group of people, and to work alongside them while we served Compassion was a dream. I remember telling our trip leader that one of my strengths would be helping to build community among us in the few days we had together. I envisioned we'd come home thick as thieves.

I was inching along the precipice I had imagined, finally ready to launch. Everything I had been working for professionally was about to pay off, and surely my personal voids would be filled and my questions would find answers . . . right?

If only . . .

TUMBLING

It can be dangerous to wander if you're on a precipice. When you get to the edge, it's all well and good if you have wings; then, you'll soar. But if you're carrying extra baggage, you're much more likely to trip and tumble.

Even before I left home for the Compassion trip, God set the stage for a glorious landslide.

18

THE PRECIPICE AND THE PIT

There is no pit so deep that God's love is not deeper still.[29]
—Corrie Ten Boom

The landslide began, innocently enough, with what I thought were seasonal allergies. As it turned out, I had a nasty head cold that would linger the entire trip. Runny-nosed and headachey, I'd have a total flight time of around twenty-two hours. Rest would have been helpful, but I wasn't able to sleep more than a few minutes on the plane. (As a snorer, I'm hyper-paranoid around strangers in such intimate quarters.)

Our plan included spending the first night in Delhi before traveling on to Kolkata. Over-stimulated from the madcap taxi ride through streets teeming with beggared people and animals, when we arrived at our hotel all I could manage was counting sheep and blessings in our windowless, pitch-black room. A few long hours later, the alarm jerked us out of bed.

On top of being sleep-deprived and feeling lousy, my personal little landslide continued in the form of culture shock. I had braced myself for the poverty we'd see, but I didn't anticipate or prepare for the daily assault to all five senses. The stench from industrial pollution mixed with open sewers punched me in the nose the second I exited our hotel; if I mouth-breathed, I could taste it. Car horns blared all night long, and the sun was a 5 a.m. alarm-bully. A heatwave kept temperatures above

100 degrees sending heat indexes soaring toward danger. Our hotel featured a beautiful, all-you-can-eat spread, but more than one dish had me literally gagging when I discovered it tasted absolutely nothing like it looked, a huge disappointment because I was so excited to experience authentic Indian fare. It took me days to figure out what foods I could tolerate, and I'm still scarred at the thought of those "poppy seed rolls" that caught my mouth on fire. Bless my American girl's heart . . . I was trying to fit into this new, exotic-to-me culture, but my body was fighting me every inch of the way.

And yet, for every sensory assault, there was a stunning grace. Because I had a cold, frequently blowing my nose helped keep my sinuses clear of the contaminants in the air (evident when I blew my nose . . . which is all I'll say about that). Our hotel provided air-conditioned relief from the sweltering heat, a luxury not afforded to most of the people we met and one I didn't take for granted. In contrast to my culinary experience at our hotel, it was a particular grace that every meal at the Compassion projects we visited was delicious, a generous offering from people who had so little to give. To me, curry still tastes like love.

We met modern-day heroes who served the children at each project. We saw how Child Survival Centers impacted women and children by providing basic nutrition, healthcare intervention, love, and support. We were invited into the homes of sponsored children who, together with their families and through a translator, explained how Compassion changed their life. Within the merciless slums of Kolkata, I found indescribable joy, hope, contentment, gratitude, peace, and love. These people knew Jesus, and it seemed because He was everything to them, they had everything they needed.

I expected to see the brutal beautiful, and I did. Poverty of this magnitude is tragically obscene, and yet God's presence in this place brought undeniable beauty.

But what I didn't expect, however, what I couldn't have prepared for, was the ugliest version of myself I've ever seen. Lurking at the bottom of the landslide was a monster, and it wasn't a lack of friendships or a bad church or a struggling writing career or a tough season of marriage. It was *me*. I came face to face with an inner, bewildering poverty of spirit that both broke my heart and infuriated me.

My first glimpse materialized when I didn't click with our team. Those lifelong friendships I imagined being forged in the slums of Kolkata never happened. No matter what I did, no matter how hard I tried, I couldn't make a meaningful connection. Everyone was polite, no one did anything wrong, but you couldn't miss the difference among those who were hitting it off. Making matters worse, as a solitary writer who needs quiet space, I didn't adjust well to group-writing around a conference table. But even when I attempted to write in that setting, I felt all alone.

Every morning I prayed for the courage to be myself, love others, make and inspire connection, maintain a positive attitude, and serve Compassion well. Every night I searched for the best words I could string together to honor this amazing organization that was changing and saving lives. But when I closed my laptop and settled in for the night, I would battle the demons whose lies bludgeoned me silly.

I was physically sick and exhausted, and never felt well from the get-go. I also felt stupid, inadequate, and like I didn't belong. It was a perfect recipe for Satan to wreak havoc in my head and heart.

I was mad . . . so blasted angry that I was wasting precious energy on myself—energy that should have been focused on our mission in India. It was maddening to be wallowing in a pool of self-pity, made even worse because I couldn't shake it off.

After all, I wasn't asked and didn't agree to travel to the other side of the world to make friends. I was there to serve. How dare I make any part of it about me or what I didn't have? I couldn't believe the absurdity of my misery. Seriously. Every day I was visiting children and their families who lived in houses the size of a walk-in closet, maybe, who weren't sure where their next meal was coming from, whose drinking water would've made me violently ill, who bathed and washed clothes in polluted streams, whose job may have earned them two dollars a day.

My head couldn't make sense of my ridiculous emotions. In one moment I was focused on helping Compassion children and their families, but in the next, I was haunted by the thought that no one cared about me—*my* talents or personality or gifts. The brutal war on my heart stood in stark contrast to such beautiful Kingdom work.

Ephesians 6:12 tells us, "For our struggle is not against flesh and blood, but against the rulers, against the authorities, against the cosmic powers of this darkness, against evil, spiritual forces in the heavens."

Mine was a deeply spiritual battle, no doubt. Was it only about flesh versus spirit? Or was there more going on? In *Waking the Dead: The Glory of a Heart Fully Alive*, John Eldredge offers an answer: "The story of your life is the story of the long and brutal assault on your heart by the one who knows what you could be and fears it."[30] Meanwhile, God's Word tells us over and over that God is for us (Rom. 8:31 and Ps. 56:9b among others).

God is for me. Satan is against me.

In my flesh versus spirit struggle in India, I was my own worst enemy (and still am at times). On top of that, there was also an enemy who understood God's claim and hope for my life, as well as His plan for my time of ministry in India. He was doing everything within his limited power to defeat me. Praise be to God for His limitless power.

The Lord was in the midst of hard and holy work, but it was just the beginning.

You always hear about the challenge of re-entry following a missions trip, and it's true. When you've spent time serving those who have so little materially—who don't have access to healthcare, education, decent jobs, and good nutrition—your heart changes, the lens through which you see the world changes. How can you reconcile the disparity between the rich and poor? You can't.

I returned home shell-shocked on two fronts and only one of them made sense to me. By sheer virtue of birth, my worries were, "What would I like to eat?" (as I stood in front of a full pantry and fridge) not "Which one of my children gets to eat today?"

"Life isn't fair" had been flipped on its head. You *know* it isn't fair that you and your family (and everyone you know) have access to clean water, good jobs, skilled doctors, dental care, free education, more food than you'll ever eat, strong shelter, reliable transportation, indoor plumbing, electricity, and a ridiculous amount of clothes and shoes.

It can be paralyzing to know you can't fix broken systems or solve world hunger or alleviate poverty once and for all. While we might know the cure for that kind of paralysis is to identify what you *can* do, and then do it, I've learned that living out what is simple can actually be rather complicated.

On top of being heartbroken over the poverty I encountered, I came home from that trip wondering what in the world was broken within me. Why had I not been able to connect well with my team? During a trip dedicated to serving others, it was incredibly disappointing and shameful to me for giving any time or thought to that lack of connection. Also, that superpower I thought I had for building community hadn't manifested itself in India, and as I looked back, it hadn't materialized in Chattanooga, either. What was I doing wrong? There was a time in my life when friendship was effortless, when I once joked about having too many friends, but my recent history told a different story, and it was painful.

No, I was no shooting star skyrocketing off a precipice. On the contrary, I had tripped and tumbled and ended up at the bottom of a landslide.

But the loveliest thing about landing in a pit is the only way out is up.

19

SURVIVAL INSTINCT

In the middle of the pouring rain / I will call your name.
When your soul sways / On and off and on again
You'll change your mind / But still be mine.[31]
Kings Kaleidoscope, "Rain"

It wasn't a big surprise to return from India deeply conflicted. But while some of the contributing reasons were anticipated— I've long heard about the difficulty of re-entry from a missions trip— some of them were not (my self-focus and inner turmoil). Remarkably, falling into a pit had placed me in a wonderful thinkin' spot.

One of humanity's strongest, most fundamental drives is our will to live. A man will go to extreme measures to ensure his survival; he will endure the unimaginable to see another day.

Consider Aron Ralston, who in 2003 went hiking alone through Utah's Blue John Canyon without informing anyone of his plans. He was descending a narrow canyon when an eight-hundred-pound boulder loosened and pinned him against the canyon wall. Over five days, he depleted his meager provisions, futilely trying to free himself from the boulder. Delirious, dehydrated, and realizing his crushed arm was already beginning to decompose, he came up with a "nothing to lose" plan to break the bones in his forearm; and then using a dull multi-tool knife, complete a crude amputation. Once freed from the boulder, he had to climb out of the canyon that held him hostage, rappel down a sixty-five-foot rock face, and then hike eight miles to his car. Luckily, he happened upon a family on vacation who helped him. Despite losing forty pounds and a quarter of his blood volume through the ordeal, he fought to stay alive.[32]

Louis Zamperini is another marvel. Coming of age during the Depression and considered to be a problem kid, he turned a corner when he discovered he could run like the wind. He made the U.S. track team for the 1936 Olympics in Berlin, and though he didn't medal, his performance was so impressive he was already considered a favorite for the 1940 Olympics. Unfortunately, World War II brought a cancellation to the games that year, and Louis ended up instead as an Air Force bombardier.

On a rescue mission over the Pacific, Louis's plane went down due to mechanical failure. Remarkably, Louis and two of his crew mates survived (one died after thirty-three days). Drifting for forty-seven days, starving, becoming dehydrated, and even fighting off sharks wouldn't be the worst of their troubles. They would be captured by the Japanese Navy and endure over two years of relentless, sadistic brutality and torture. Initially struggling after his release and return home, at the urging of his wife he attended a Billy Graham Crusade where he recommitted his life to Christ. He went on to become an evangelist and a champion of forgiveness. He, too, fought to stay alive.

When I was in high school, I was certified to be a lifeguard. I still remember the strong cautions by our instructors to "Reach, Throw, Row, Go," a prescribed order for safe rescue of a drowning victim. We were advised only to enter the water ourselves as a last resort because it was the most dangerous approach of all. Someone who's drowning, they explained, is panicked and irrational. They will grab onto anything or anyone in an effort to save themselves. This is why we read headlines about double drownings; the initial victim, in a frenzied attempt to save his life, will push his rescuer underwater to gain "footing" to breathe. People fight to the end if they're drowning.

Our human instinct is for self-preservation, doing whatever is necessary to live another day.

We do this in our spiritual lives, too. Though we've been told to lay down our lives, to die to our old self, we fight to stay alive, to keep making "provision for the flesh" (Rom. 13:14 ESV). We may say that we're willing to put an end to the old self and crucify the flesh, but when Satan tempts us otherwise or when our human nature gasps for air, do our lives demonstrate what we profess? Or do we, like someone who is drowning, push everyone else around us down—even our would-be rescuer—fighting to let the old self gulp just one more breath?

Do we look that different from the world? Or are we governed by survival instinct, our old self forcing its way back into our lives? In the upside-down world of God's Kingdom, we're called to follow Jesus, and following Jesus means picking up a cross, denying ourselves, and following Him to our deaths. Each of the gospel writers understood how important it was for us to hear these words from Jesus over and over again:

> Then Jesus said to his disciples, "If anyone wants to follow after me, let him deny himself, take up his cross, and follow me. For whoever wants to save his life will lose it, but whoever loses his life because of me will find it. For what will it benefit someone if he gains the whole world yet loses his life? Or what will anyone give in exchange for his life?" (Matt. 16:24–26)

> Calling the crowd along with his disciples, he said to them, "If anyone wants to follow after me, let him deny himself, take up his cross, and follow me. For whoever wants to save his life will lose it, but whoever loses his life because of me and the gospel will save it. For what does it benefit someone to gain the whole world and yet lose his life?" (Mark 8:34–36)

Then he said to them all, "If anyone wants to follow after me, let him deny himself, take up his cross daily, and follow me. For whoever wants to save his life will lose it, but whoever loses his life because of me will save it. For what does it benefit someone if he gains the whole world, and yet loses or forfeits himself?" (Luke 9:23–25)

"The one who loves his life will lose it, and the one who hates his life in this world will keep it for eternal life." (John 12:25)

This idea, this command, isn't limited to the gospel writers. We find it all over the New Testament:

I have been crucified with Christ, and I no longer live, but Christ lives in me. The life I now live in the body, I live by faith in the Son of God, who loved me and gave himself for me. (Gal. 2:20)

For you died, and your life is hidden with Christ in God. (Col. 3:3)

How can we who died to sin still live in it? Or are you unaware that all of us who were baptized into Christ Jesus were baptized into his death? Therefore we were buried with him by baptism into death, in order that, just as Christ was raised from the dead by the glory of the Father, so we too may walk in newness of life. For if we have been united with him in the likeness of his death, we will certainly also be in the likeness of his resurrection. For we know that our old self was crucified with him so that the body ruled by sin might be rendered powerless so that we may no longer be enslaved to sin, since a person who has died is freed from sin. Now if we died with Christ, we believe that we will also live with him, because we know that Christ, having been raised from the dead, will not die again. Death no longer rules over him. For the death he died, he died to sin once for all time; but the life he lives, he lives to God. So, you too consider yourselves dead to sin and alive to God in Christ Jesus. (Rom. 6:2–11)

Therefore, if anyone is in Christ, he is a new creation; the old has passed away, and see, the new has come! (2 Cor. 5:17)

. . . take off your former way of life, the old self that is corrupted by deceitful desires, to be renewed in the spirit of your minds, and to put on the new self, the one created according to God's likeness in righteousness and purity of the truth. (Eph. 4:22–24)

These passages are by no means exhaustive, but they are telling. Who we are after coming to faith should look very different than before. As we mature as believers, our responses to life, to hardship, to daily tasks, to *everything*, should become increasingly Christlike.

I'm convinced all my struggles in life are inextricably intertwined with my faith. And despite everything I had learned over a lifetime in church, regardless of all the head knowledge I had acquired, no matter the Truth I believed to be true, I was drowning in my faith. Had the old Robin been

> As we mature as believers, our responses to life, to hardship, to daily tasks, to *everything*, should become increasingly Christlike.

trying to drown the new Robin all these years? Did I have help from my worst enemy, also eager to push the new Robin under, so the old Robin could keep breathing? There was no way I could have been "fixing [my] eyes on Jesus, the source and perfecter of our faith" (Heb. 12:2 NIV); I was too still too aware of and focused on myself.

Thinking my self-reliance, resourcefulness, and hard work—my flesh—were compatible with who God calls me to be in Christ, I didn't fully understand they weren't a life vest to help me float at all; they were concrete blocks pulling me under. I was drowning, when all Jesus wanted to do was save me from myself. That's who He is, our saver, our *Savior*. When any of His children are drowning, all Jesus wants to do is rescue us. He was willing to give His life for me, even in my worst moments when I felt like a monster—even when I was wandering around in a pit. But I wasn't willing to do the same. I clung to my life. The old Robin in me had been fighting to live, and the new Robin, with the help of her worst enemy, wasn't putting up much of a fight.

20

HELD

So deeply rooted in our hearts is unbelief, so prone are we to it, that while all confess with the lips that God is faithful, no man ever believes it without an arduous struggle.[33]
—John Calvin, *Institutes of the Christian Religion*

When you're wandering in a spiritual desert, or at the bottom of a spiritual pit, or drowning in a spiritual sea, or whatever you want to call it, one thing is for certain: you feel so alone. What I didn't believe, and what you need to know if you find yourself in this place, is that you *aren't* actually alone. Just like when I was little and thought I was lost at the county fair, what we feel and think may not be the case at all.

Remember: Just because it feels like you're all alone doesn't mean you are. There are others struggling just like you, and most important, God is with you.

> Remember: Just because it feels like you're all alone doesn't mean you are.

During your season of wandering, perhaps you never lost a sense of God's presence; or possibly you felt the opposite, abandoned in the desert. Whichever the case, it is always helpful to hear the experience of another, isn't it? To help you feel a little less crazy, a little less lonely, and maybe a little more hopeful that God understands, that He's not threatened or offended, and He knows just what you need.

In fact, these moments of wandering and doubt and confusion are actually an evidence of God *at work in* you, not His abandoning you. Isn't that a revolutionary, almost scandalous thought? It flips struggling with unbelief on its head and disarms the strength of an enemy who is always and only against us.

> Knowing that God is at work in you flips struggling with unbelief on its head and disarms the strength of an enemy who is always and only against you.

Parsing out the tensions of our faith is part of the growth process. As Barnabas Piper says, doubt isn't really the enemy of faith, it's a catalyst for it. When reading Barnabas's experience with that famous phrase in Mark 9, "I believe, help my unbelief," I felt a little less alone, and a little more understood. Maybe this internal battle, this wandering, this ruthless and unending tension was *normal* after all:

> In my mid-twenties, I went through what rightly could be called a crisis of faith—a true test of whether I should devote my life to what I grew up believing about Jesus. I was faced with the decision of walking away from it all, because that would be the easier thing to do, or turning to Jesus and giving Him all of my life. . . .
>
> For most of my life I had felt the pull, the tension of faith. . . . I believed in Jesus, but I doubted. I believed in Jesus, but I didn't. Then one day I stumbled across this story from Mark. I'd read it dozens of times, but this time it grabbed me. That one sentence grabbed me.
>
> The father's words gripped my heart with a viselike power. In five words he explained so much of the Christian

experience, of my experience. That simple sentence is the key to the struggles, the ups and downs, the winding road of belief. In a breath he expressed the highest of heights, the strength of virtue, the emptiness of doubt, and the yearning for something on to which he could hold. He spoke of being pulled in two opposite directions, one of peace and the other of chaos and fear. And he spoke of clinging, holding fast, knowing to whom he should look. All this in five little words.

Christians who don't know the tension of "I believe; help my unbelief" might not be Christians at all, or at the least they might be very infantile ones. Our faith is one of brutal tensions. Not everyone can express this, but every Christian knows it. We feel it in our guts. We feel as if we're going to bust in half as we're pulled in two directions at once. To not recognize the significance of these words indicates a simplistic, thoughtless belief. It isn't a mark of maturity but rather of not being mature enough to know our own weakness and need. Tension is our state of being for all of this life, and to live as a believer is to live in it.[34]

The mere act of someone else understanding makes a difference.

My wrestling match with unbelief seemed to come from nowhere and everywhere. Though it didn't feel like they were connected, I suspect the difficulties of moving to a new place, of starting over, of feeling marginalized and dismissed, of my age and measure of success, of the church debacles—of the monster of myself—were all dubious "evidences" against the idea that God was really there for me, or even there at all.

Bringing our darkness into the light diffuses its strength. It may not resolve our doubts and questions to admit them out loud to someone who loves us no matter what, but somehow it minimizes their power over us or makes them a little less frightening. Sensing this, I finally mustered the courage to admit my doubts to Tad. I told him while I felt like a Judeo-Christian ethic was the best framework for raising our children, I wasn't sure if I even believed in God at all. I explained that some things I had long-professed I no longer believed and maybe never had.

Tad's left-brain response was perfectly on par with who I've always known him to be, holding nothing back and calling things as he saw them: "Well, I don't see you doing anything about it"—essentially telling me I was reaping exactly what I was sowing. He wasn't emotional or alarmed or condemning; he already knew I wasn't digging into my faith. He was simply pointing out that I didn't seem to be seeking God for answers, and that I wasn't doing anything to work through or resolve my questions.

And he was right. I *wasn't* doing anything about it. The old Robin had been drowning the new one for a long, long while, and the new Robin hadn't been fighting back, oblivious she was even in a fight at all.

Well, hmph. That didn't seem particularly helpful. But, trusting his insight I decided to make an effort to "do." I was hoping if my behavior changed, maybe my feelings—and my faith—would follow. Honestly, I was skeptical it would make a difference.

In a small act of obedience, I began praying. I should explain that even throughout years of wandering spiritually, I had never stopped praying altogether. But these prayers were different. Though they felt mechanical, like I was talking to air, they were gut-level honest. Praying out loud, sitting at my kitchen table feeling every bit a fool, I told God I didn't know if I believed He was real. If He was real, I needed Him to convince me.

I was no longer willing to profess something I didn't believe. I could no longer accept the prescribed faith of my youth, my church, our culture or anyone around me. If I was going to continue in this thing called faith, God was going to have to make Himself known or I was done.

And then something began happening during this season of prayer, something I didn't expect, and something for which I was too short-sided to ask: God began transforming me and literally changing the way I was thinking. It wasn't overnight, but it was obvious. I know how I think, and I noticed when thought patterns started shifting. There is no greater evidence of God at work in this world than a changed mind that leads to a changed life . . . and my life was changing from the inside out.

> There is no greater evidence of God at work in this world than a changed mind that leads to a changed life . . .

In an incredible demonstration of His kindness, patience, and faithfulness, God began revealing more of Himself to me as His love for me changed how I viewed others and how I saw myself in relation to them. Sometimes He showed up in what I call "Godwinks," the sort of things some people chalk up to coincidence but instead tell me He really knows me and genuinely cares for me. Sometimes when I opened my Bible, a passage would speak directly into my circumstances. I strongly sensed His presence as we began to worship in a new place.

I've never heard God speak audibly, but when I was dangerously teetering toward unbelief, He gave me a vivid image of His faithfulness. My mind's eye sees it as fresh today as it did the first time I saw it: nearing the end of my spiritual rope and close to opening my hand to let go, God reached out, gripped my wrist, and held tight.

A veil was lifted and I could finally see: *God's* faithfulness has nothing to do with *mine.*

Oh, friend, I feel the need to stop here to say if you need encouragement today, know this: the Bible is telling the truth when it says that if you pray, God will give you more of Himself, and that if you find yourself faithless, God will remain faithful (Luke 11:13; 2 Tim. 2:13).

God's faithfulness is not contingent on yours.

If you've just stepped into a season of doubt and aimlessness, God is there. Or if it's been years of the back and forth and you're wandering in circles: God is there, too. If you're at the end of your rope, He's not letting go. You are His, chosen and beloved. He is a God who keeps His covenant to us, and—*praise God!*—His faithfulness is not contingent on yours. If you're on the edge of a precipice or in the middle of a landslide, you'll eventually end up just like me. *Held tightly.*

That you are wrestling confirms that God is working.

Because, ever faithful, God moves on our behalf. That you are wrestling confirms that God is working. Whether you're failing or faithless or floundering or falling, He's holding onto you. The especially good news is He never lets go.

21

LIFELINES

Miracles are a retelling in small letters of the very
same story which is written across the whole world
in letters too large for some of us to see.[35]
—C. S. Lewis, *God in the Dock*

Matthew 6:33 is my father-in-law's life verse, the verse he nestles right under his name when he sends me (and anyone else) a card or note. This has been his practice for as long as I can remember.

Early on, I wasn't that impressed with his choice because it seemed so, well . . . common, almost like a foregone conclusion for anyone who called themselves a Christian. Surely, he could have chosen a Scripture more complex and theologically challenging than plain old ". . . seek ye first the kingdom of God, and his righteousness; and all these things shall be added unto you" (always King James, his preferred version of Scripture). That verse didn't seem special enough, or no—deep enough—for someone of his spiritual depth and maturity. *Surely* he could have found a more original or pro-found verse hidden somewhere in the Scriptures. Then, again, I was younger and I knew "so much more" then than I do now.

> God isn't in the business of keeping Himself from us.

Only when I began wholeheartedly seeking God did I understand the depth and beauty of this command and its incalculable promises. I found out, as I'm sure he did long ago, its truth is foundational to faith. Tommy's life verse plainly explains that seeking God is the remedy to anxiety, and it's linked to His sufficiency and provision for our needs. As I examined other verses about seeking God, one truth became very apparent: God isn't in the business of keeping Himself from us. God wants to be found:

> I love those who love me, and those who search for me find me. (Prov. 8:17)

> You will seek me and find me when you search for me with all your heart. (Jer. 29:13)

> Seek the Lord while he may be found; call to him while he is near. (Isa. 55:6)

> Draw near to God, and he will draw near to you. (James 4:8a)

If we're earnestly looking for God, we're going to find Him; in the Bible, of course, but also in the lives of other believers, in creation, in art and music, and the giftings of ordinary people living out their calling.

If we're earnestly looking for God, we're going to find Him.

But sometimes when our faith goes sideways, we need God to show up anyway. We need Him to come to us, even when we're not necessarily looking for Him. Remarkably, He's more than willing. After all He did this very thing in the incarnation— when He left heaven, became a human, and came to our broken world in a way no one expected, as a king born in poverty. Everything about Jesus' coming was a miracle.

Sometimes we receive an assurance from God—a lifeline, a Godwink, or even a flat-out miracle—that indicates He sees us, knows us, loves us, and notices and cares about our broken places and emptiness. Sometimes He is generous to give us something we need whether or not we asked, and even if we aren't convinced the "I Am" even *is*. When we are struggling or even walking away, God can show up in unexpected ways.

When I was drowning, when I entertained the idea of letting go of my faith, God held onto me. *He* reached for *me*, not the other way around. In fact, looking back over my life, I see that God did this on more than one occasion, in big ways and small. His faithfulness showed up again and again, sometimes in ways I couldn't necessarily see until later.

When my wilderness was new and disorienting, God threw me a lifeline in a Sunday morning sermon, showing up despite my wrestle with belief. It was a few years after moving to Tennessee, when John was still our pastor. I didn't know or care if that sermon meant a thing to anyone else in the room, it was me and God and God and me that morning, and the hope it offered would become a thread tethering my faith for years as it drifted.

That morning my pastor explained that if you were struggling with unbelief, it didn't mean you weren't saved. God wasn't caught off guard by our questions and He wasn't offended by our doubt. But the kicker, the inspired message that gave me the hope I would cling to in my spiritual desert, was John's suggestion that God could actually be using my doubt and questions as the means to woo me back to His side. Rather than heaping guilt or condemnation on my already sagging shoulders, he lifted my chin as if to say "Everything's going to be alright."

Rather than viewing my questions as a sinister divide between me and God, I began seeing them as a bridge. Question by question, slat by slat, my doubts were bringing me closer to truth, not driving me away. Wandering doesn't always mean you're leaving God; sometimes you're just taking the long way home.

Reframing my questions in a positive light, as both a vehicle for God's grace and a means for me to seek Him was a game changer. It didn't immediately quell my doubts—again, this was early in my wandering—but it extended the freedom for me to be honest, wrestle, and find a way back to Truth.

> Wandering doesn't always mean you're leaving God; sometimes you're just taking the long way home.

Another time, on one of those days when my doubts felt more real than Truth, I slammed my fist on my kitchen table and demanded a sign from God to show me He was real. Oh, my, the nerve I had in that moment! Despite my presumptuousness, God showed up and tossed me another lifeline, keeping me afloat when I felt like I was drowning.

That very afternoon when I walked down the driveway to check our mail, I had a letter from a friend I hadn't heard from in years. Rhonda was one of my faithful Sunday morning nursery volunteers, and both of her children had attended the Parents Morning Out program I had served as director. For two pages she thanked me for my service, making note of details I had long forgotten. The little things mattered to her, and she noticed and remembered them. She told me how she had seen Jesus in my life, and how that had impacted her own faith. At the end of the note she casually mentioned she was ill and she asked me to pray for her. Not long after I received her letter, she died from a brain tumor.

She had no way of knowing when she wrote it, that three days later I would be desperate to know God was even real. God, ever faithful, knew. Her letter was an answer to prayer, an evidence of God Himself. I was so heartened by the perfect timing. This felt like a loving Father winking and smiling at His daughter as He reassured her and gave her exactly what she had asked for.

And then there was the miracle of the baby rainbow. I bet you didn't even know there was such a thing. It arrived on a day when it was storming inside and out, when my heart was bullied and bruised by the equivalent of a paper cut, a small sort of worry that demanded ridiculously more than its share of attention. Logically, I knew I was making a big deal out of something that shouldn't have carried so much weight, but I couldn't shake it. I had been marginalized in my blogging world by someone I had trusted, and the omission felt like betrayal, as painful as it was surprising. Outside the rain was soothing as it tapered to a drizzle but thunder captured the emotion of my heart.

I sat at our kitchen bar and stared out the window into the backyard, fighting back tears and struggling to complete a writing project. I was so angry to be sad over "nothing," but I couldn't pull myself together. I was lost in my own head, the fog so thick I hadn't even realized it when Stephen, my youngest, walked into the room behind me to announce the miracle:

"Mom, there's a baby rainbow in our front yard!" He had to say it twice to clear the haze.

I whipped around to look out the front window to realize he meant exactly what he said. There was a tiny rainbow stretched across our front yard, starting on one side of our driveway and arching toward the woods. I grabbed my camera, flew out the front door, and managed to capture a few images before it faded. I had been staring in the wrong direction—my gaze fixated on the backyard instead of the front, focused on the rain when one of nature's most beautiful spectacles was right behind me. Had Stephen not walked down at that very moment, I would have missed one of the most amazing sights I've ever seen. And I *needed* to see it.

We all know what rainbows represent in the Bible—a promise that God would not flood the earth again. Rainbows are God's way of reminding us that though the rains will come, He is with us before, during, and after the storm. They are an evidence of God's presence and an expression of His faithfulness, mercy, love, and covenant promise to us. It is no wonder, then, that I was overwhelmed. I remain certain this rainbow was for me, an incredible gift from God for His daughter. Sharing it with Stephen—someone who would appreciate it as much as me—was icing on the cake. In a moment when I felt forgotten and unworthy, God showed me otherwise: I am known and loved.

What a gift, each of these lifelines. God knowing the state of my heart—wrestling and wandering—and yet *still* graciously revealing Himself to me. Whether I was demanding or doubting or devoid of the good sense to ask at all, He was faithful to make Himself known. Even when I felt like He was nowhere to be found, God proved that none of that mattered because *He* knew *me*.

Just like the moment in my kitchen before Stephen told me about the tiny rainbow, there might be times I've missed seeing God when I wasn't looking for Him. But the good news is this: *He is always looking for me,* waiting for the perfect moment to meet the desperate needs of my heart, eager for me to see Him.

The same is true for you, sweet friend.

22

TORNADO

When the roots are deep,
there is no reason to fear the wind.[36]
—Ancient Proverb

Years after the sermon about doubt and the letter from my dying friend and the baby rainbow, God sent me another lifeline. But before I recognized it was a gift, I literally thought it might kill me.

The visit to my in-laws had been on my calendar for weeks and I wasn't about to let a little bad weather thwart my plans, though "bad weather" might have been an understatement. The entire Southeast was under watches and warnings as a wicked tropical storm bullied its way from the Gulf Coast to the Atlantic.

I had toyed with the idea of postponing my trip, but with my mother-in-law's dementia and declining health, my desire to help and spend time with my father-in-law outweighed my concern about poor weather or road conditions. Sometimes stupidity trumps reason when the heart is involved.

The trip is about four hours on a good day and you can choose one of two very different routes: Speed northwest through Atlanta and zip east toward South Carolina, fifty-five miles longer but interstate the whole way; or trim the mileage and opt for a slower tempo, two lanes threading together one small town after another, a rural northeast trek.

A quick comparison on my GPS app indicated substantially less driving time if I chose the option that sent me through Atlanta. Never mind the future weather radar I also checked, aflame in blotches of red and orange. There was potential for violent weather in both directions so why not get there as soon as I could? Plus, weather forecasters don't always get it right, but those treacherous predictions sure boost ratings and page views. Maybe they were just exaggerating to keep us glued to their updates.

I was forty-five minutes into my drive when my cell phone rang. Leave it to my dear husband to get in my business. Even before I answered the phone, I knew why he was calling. Aware I was in for rough weather, he had been studying the future forecast and determined the best option was *not* through Atlanta. Though we hadn't talked since he left for work earlier that morning, and he didn't know for sure what time I was getting on the road or which way I was headed, he knows me well enough to make an educated guess that I'd go with the shortest route . . . and he didn't agree or approve.

The future weather model predicted that the worst of the storm would follow me straight up the interstate along the shorter way. Tad strongly cautioned me to change my course as soon as I could. Irritated because I cared more about drive time and less about the weather, but also knowing he was probably right given what I had seen on the weather channel myself, I pulled off at the next exit, recalculated my navigation, and started in the other direction.

In front of me the sky brightened while behind me an ominous cauldron simmered in my rearview mirror. I grudgingly conceded that Tad was right and this was the better way. Nevertheless, I respected the forecast I had been hearing about all week, and to keep apprised of changing weather and warnings, I tuned my radio to a local station. When I'd get out of range, I'd find another.

This went on swimmingly for a while until, wouldn't you know it, the weathermen were proven right. Conditions deteriorated. Menacing clouds crept across the sky. A haphazard drizzle developed into steady rain. My radio squealed and squawked watches and warnings, more annoying than anything else because the rain really wasn't that big of a deal. I figured my path must have been skirting the fringe of more problematic weather, near enough to warrant a local warning, but never in my purview. Still, since I couldn't exactly drive and keep an eye on my phone's radar, I kept the radio on. The severe weather alerts eventually sounded like boys crying wolf to me, any sense of urgency dulling from their frequency.

A spiritual parallel came to mind—God is so right about His people's hard-headedness—sometimes hearing what we *really* need to hear over and over still doesn't change our minds or hearts. If anything, it somehow makes us pay less attention instead of more. With my current situation, there was a disconnect between those obnoxious alarms on the radio, real danger, and what I could see with my own eyes. "Much ado about nothing," I mused. "April showers bring May flowers." No one else on the road seemed concerned, either. More than a few drivers seemed to think they were on the NASCAR circuit despite slick pavement.

It was a relief to get off the interstate when I finally reached my exit. I had about an hour and a half remaining to my in-laws, and, thankfully, the rest of my drive was on a two-lane road, an easy ramble through the country. No more rude eighteen-wheelers chomping at my bumper, no more cars jerking into my lane when their foolish drivers texted illegally in the rain.

It had been years since I had traveled this route, and I appreciated every familiar landmark that welcomed me back. Even in the rain it was a prettier ride than the interstate. I didn't realize how tense I had become driving in traffic while anticipating a torrential downpour that never quite materialized. I exhaled, relaxed, and my mind wandered.

I didn't notice when the sky began to darken.

Lost in thought, I hadn't realized the dramatic change in atmosphere, my senses lulled from the monotony of driving. My brain was having difficulty reconciling what I was seeing, the same way there's a delay in understanding when you think you're drinking unsweet tea but you accidentally reach for someone's Coke (or worse, expecting fresh chocolate milk out of one of those tiny pint cartons only to discover it's sour. *That* was the day I learned all about expiration dates. Happened in sixth grade and I haven't recovered yet.). It takes a second or two, but then suddenly you understand what is going on.

The preternatural sky intensified, an inky slate resembling a solar eclipse. Geeking into amateur meteorologist mode, I so admired its beauty I couldn't help myself—I had to take a picture. It was easy to rationalize. Traffic wasn't an issue and it was barely dribbling outside. I patted around the console next to my seat until I found my phone and then carefully raised it to rest on my steering wheel. Never taking my eyes off the road, I balanced the phone with both hands, aimed skyward as best I could, and starting tapping. I wouldn't know until later whether or not I managed to capture anything of value, so I kept clicking and pivoting my phone until I was satisfied the odds were in my favor. Mission hopefully accomplished, I tossed my phone on the passenger-side seat.

Figuratively speaking, don't we sometimes do this in life and faith? Observe a storm from a distance and only see its wonder and majesty, an opportunity for God to show up and show off, displaying His sovereignty and omnipotence? But, that is when the storm is in *someone else's* life, and we are inspired and even encouraged to see God's hand at work. We may not get out our iPhones to take a picture but we stand back and marval from a position of safety instead of recognizing someone else's storm is a chance for us to prepare.

So, here I was, still not comprehending I was in the center of a weather event that could literally rip me apart, *taking a picture*. As is often the case with tempests in life, it never occurred to me I should be *preparing* for what was about to happen, not taking a stupid picture of it.

On the turn of a dime it (finally) occurred to me that something was dreadfully wrong. No matter how lovely or unusual, a midday sky shouldn't be all soot and shadows. It was eerie and dark and haunting—too still—not to be raining, too. *Where was all the rain? Wasn't this a storm?* As I abruptly snapped out of my trance, everything happened at once—

I felt a slight tickling sensation all over my body, like the hairs on my arms were standing on end and someone was lightly passing their hand across them. Electric. And terrifying. Suddenly and savagely, rain and hail poured down and pelted my car by the bucketload. Though safe inside, I still ducked and flinched under their machine-gun assault. My car swayed and swerved at the mercy of wind and water, and I white-knuckled my steering wheel. Serious concentration was required just to stay in my lane or to see the road at all. A weather alert shrieked from my radio, a different alert, the one with apocalyptic warning:

> *The National Weather Service has issued a tornado warning in your area . . . extremely dangerous . . . life threatening . . . capable of producing golfball-size hail and destructive straight-line winds . . . take cover now . . . cars and mobile homes should be abandoned for sturdier shelter . . .*

I scoured the landscape looking for any sign of a dark funnel but lanky pines and tall oaks lined the rural highway, obscuring the view on both sides. I studied the reflection in my rearview and side mirrors but they stared back gray and impassive. The radio urged me to seek shelter but houses were few and far between, and every one I passed looked like it might blow away any minute too.

I was petrified. I felt like an animal cornered by an invisible beast who was having fun playing with his prey, waiting to devour him when he got bored. *Bird Box* all over again.

My heart was a jackhammer and my body a quaking mess. I inched along the highway, eyes darting back and forth, back and forth, willing shelter to appear out of nowhere. I scanned the shoulders of the road looking for a ditch while wondering if anyone had ever actually been saved that way. Was I really willing to lie prostrate in a puddle of mud, roadside garbage, and who knows what else, with my hands covering the back of my head, and what would it feel like for those monster pines to fall across my back?

I actually wondered if this was going to be how I died.

"Jesus," I whispered, "Jesus, Jesus, Jesus," desperate, faster . . . louder. All I could say, all I could pray, was "Jesus" a thousand times over. Hunched down in my seat (as if that would help), clinging to my steering wheel, there was only one word on my lips.

I wondered if my last word on earth might be my first one in heaven.

I have no idea how long I had been driving—five minutes might as well have been forever—when I passed a sign that read "Persimmon Hill Golf Club" and below that, "Public Welcome." I accepted their kind invitation by barreling my car through the entrance like a bull chasing red. Hoping that its restaurant or pro shop would be open, I added two words to my "Jesus" broken record when I spotted other cars in the parking lot. *Thank You.*

I disregarded the law and swerved into the empty handicapped parking spot closest to the building. I couldn't imagine anyone needing that space would be foolish enough to be out in the weather, and if they were, they would've pulled right up to the wheelchair ramp, anyway. The location of the parking spot required you to go backwards and then around a safety rail, essentially doubling the distance between your car and the door.

Frantically unbuckling my seat belt, I twisted over my seat to fish an umbrella from the floorboard behind me. It was still pouring rain and hail, a million tiny ping pong balls were ricocheting off my hood in every direction.

The wind put up a nasty fight when I opened my car door, and instantly I was soaked. Undeterred, I scurried around the safety rail toward the building's entrance while simultaneously pressing the button on my umbrella to open it automatically. Its dome opened and slammed backwards, but as I instinctively turned toward the wind, it blew into shape and offered at least some protection from the hail. I was surprised but thankful to see how tiny it actually was—pea- to marble-size. From inside my car it had sounded like basketballs and boulders.

I couldn't see beyond the glass door as I reached for the knob, but never have I been more thankful than when it opened with ease. I stepped inside to safety, and would've kneeled and kissed the ground had it not been for three golfers casually standing around with beer in hand.

Drenched but relieved I asked, "Is the tornado nearby?" and one of the guys answered flatly, "You're right under it." Another was on his phone and reported it had just touched down a block or two from where we were. Something about how calm they were WHEN A TORNADO WAS ON TOP OF US didn't seem right. But it was also reassuring—if they weren't worrying, why should I? Maybe this little brick building was stronger than it looked.

It was obvious I was rattled, so they suggested I might want to join the "others." Directing me to an interior, concrete block-lined hallway, I discovered four grandmothers sitting in a row, patiently waiting for the storm to pass so they could get back to more important things (their bridge game). I excused myself first to the restroom to towel off and try to regain an ounce of composure, and then returned to my new friends. As I recounted my experience, they told me there wasn't another business around for miles either way. "Well aren't you lucky?" but I knew luck had nothing to do with it.

Jesus, indeed.

Thirty minutes later I was back on the road and made it to my in-laws without further incident. That night I scoured the internet for information. Traveling just over seven miles with wind speeds reaching 115 mph, the tornado snapped and uprooted trees, damaged cars, homes, and businesses—but somehow, miraculously, not a single person was harmed. I eventually discovered it was an EF-2, not the worst level of tornado, but certainly one that could stir up trouble.

Never have I been more frightened. I certainly can't recall another time I believed my life was in imminent danger. I'm sure you've heard the old war adage, "There are no atheists in foxholes," something I've thought about in relation to my experience that day. What would a person with no faith say or think in the same situation? Would he curse the storm and that be that? Would she bargain with God if He spared her life only to forget her promise once safe? Might it be the very thing to break through walls and chains and bondage to open the eyes of a heart to finally see and hear and respond to the call of God?

I *have* to believe in deathbed conversions, that God does not grow weary, and He longs for us to find Him, to accept what He's offered, that He doesn't put limits on when or how that might happen. After all, the criminal dying next to Jesus dared to be remembered by Him, and he was. What astonishing evidence that it is never too late to respond to the gospel, as long as you draw breath. "It is never too late" reserves space for great hope.

> It is never too late to respond to the gospel.

My husband and I have played a kind of game through the years, a constructive exercise for intentional living. For lack of an actual name let's call it *What would we do if we were in their shoes?* When tragedy or trying circumstances struck in the lives of people in our sphere, we'd ask ourselves how we might respond—how we *hoped* we would respond—if the same thing happened to us. How would we want to respond if . . . we couldn't have children, we unexpectedly lost a loved one, one of us received a terminal diagnosis, we were a casualty of downsizing, we couldn't afford to pay our bills. The list is endless, the things in life threatening to batter or break us. Each incident that affected those around us provided personal opportunity to consider, maybe even plan with intention, how we'd want to respond if we found ourselves in a similar position.

Our reactions are telling, aren't they? How we respond reveals the measure of our faith and what we understand about the character of God. Our responses are an indicator of spiritual maturity, how well we know God, and what we believe about Him.

I think those who wander in their faith like me, who haven't yet managed to resolve all doubt, can take an experience like this as a gift from God. In the tornado, I had this rare opportunity to see how I'd respond when faced with a possible threat to my life. That Jesus was my immediate thought, cry, prayer, and plea is an ongoing source of encouragement to me, even now.

Storms reveal who we really trust when we're pushed beyond our breaking points. And though I had been wandering off and on for so many years, the tornado showed me that deep down, at the end of it all, I really did trust Jesus.

> Storms reveal who we really trust when we're pushed beyond our breaking points.

Who knew that a potentially life-threatening natural disaster could be a lifeline? In the midst of this harrowing experience, I got a glimpse of how I'd respond when faced with imminent danger, and that would be to cry out for Jesus. God isn't just faithful in hard times, His Holy Spirit is *in* us all the time, just waiting for opportunities to reveal Himself. I didn't even realize how much I needed to know that, how a moment of fear could be transformed into faith because of Christ in me.

And much as I disdain those Sunday school answers, I'll be darned if they aren't right sometimes. Jesus, the only word on my lips when I was scared half to death, was, indeed, the perfect response.

23

IT'S A WONDERFUL LIFE

Strange, isn't it? Each man's life touches so many other lives.
When he isn't around he leaves an awful hole, doesn't he?[37]
—Clarence to George Bailey, *It's a Wonderful Life*

One of the greatest dangers when you're wandering in a spiritual desert is losing your sense of direction, your North Star, your purpose, your *raison d'être*. You're grasping at things the world has to offer, but this is futile; your problem is deeply spiritual. You can't cure disease with an impotent, incompatible remedy.

I've *tsked-tsked* Israel before, shaking my head over her foolishness after being rescued from captivity. How in the world could a group of people who had seen all they saw—plagues and miracles and Red Sea parting, *oh, my!*—fall into disobedience, struggle with belief, and end up wandering around in circles for forty years? (Read Exodus 7–16 for a refresher.) Could the Israelites have lost their sense of direction because somehow they forgot God's faithfulness to them? It seems to me, Israel didn't wander because they didn't know where they were going; they wandered because they took their eyes off of the one leading them. *And it bore grievous consequences.*

If that ain't a cautionary tale, I don't know what is.

When I think about my own sin and disobedience, my reckless, careless ways, and my stubborn, willful, self-reliant heart, it's a wonder God has been so patient and long-suffering with me. That He hasn't given up on me gives me hope. That I'm still in this world tells me there's still work to be done in me, and more exciting, still work for me to do in this world and opportunity to bring glory to God.

The same is true for you.

If you have any doubt that your life is making a difference in this world, if you're having trouble believing God has unique plans for *your* life, or if you're struggling with your self-worth, you need to understand that you are not here by chance. When you consider all the factors that preceded your conception and birth, the number of contingencies absolutely necessary in order to make one person out of two, it's a miracle to have been born. Did you know that the probability of you or me existing at all is 1 in $10^{2,685,000}$? That's a ten with enough zeros after it to emulsify your brain. Or as one expert would put it, "It's the probability of 2 million people getting together—about the population of San Diego—each to play a game of dice with trillion-sided dice. They each roll the dice, and they all come up the exact same number—say, 550,343,279,001."[38]

(Math, you slay me.)

Your life, your very existence, is incredible when you take the time to linger in the wonder of it. If your mama had a headache that night or your daddy had a lousy day at work, you might not have been at all.

Are you getting this? A unique array of circumstances shackled to the genesis of creation set off a chain reaction that eventually led to you. I can't even begin to wrap my head around all this—the odds suggest it is exponentially more likely for you not to have been born.

But God knew. Before time as we know it began, He planned you, He made plans for you, and He is intimately acquainted with everything about you. You've heard these Scriptures, but do you believe them for yourself? Has familiarity bred contempt or sown indifference?

> For it was you who created my inward parts; you knit me together in my mother's womb. I will praise you because I have been remarkably and wondrously made. Your works

are wondrous, and I know this very well. My bones were not hidden from you when I was made in secret, when I was formed in the depths of the earth. Your eyes saw me when I was formless; all my days were written in your book and planned before a single one of them began. (Ps. 139:13–16)

"I chose you before I formed you in the womb; I set you apart before you were born." (Jer. 1:5)

Everything about you matters, my friend, because God made you on purpose. You are no afterthought, you are set apart for God's glory, created to do what only you can accomplish. God isn't in the business of making people just to pass time; we're created for a reason. You are the only You this world will ever have, and your life and presence matters because you're impacting everyone and everything around you.

Now, I think our tendency is to think only our "good" parts will be of benefit to others—our strengths, our successes, our positive experiences. But isn't God's an upside-down Kingdom where few things arrive as expected? What if it is our short-comings or the ugly parts we'd rather keep to ourselves that are the very instruments God is using to conform us to the image of Christ and minister to those around us? My friend, Hannah, says it this way: "People are impressed by our strengths but drawn to us (and therefore Jesus) in our weakness." Folks don't need to see the pretty highlight reels of our lives; they're encouraged when they realize they aren't the only one struggling in life and faith.

> The ugly parts we'd rather keep to ourselves are the very instruments God is using to conform us to the image of Christ.

I'm a big fan of the movies *It's a Wonderful Life* starring Jimmy Stewart, *Back to the Future* with Michael J. Fox, and *The Family Man* with Nicolas Cage. Do you know what they all have in common? They each tell the story of what could have been if the main character had made different choices in their past. Each protagonist gets to catch a glimpse of the ripple effects that would have happened if he made alternative decisions. My favorite is *It's a Wonderful Life* because we see, for George Bailey, what could have been isn't as good as what *is*.

We all face forks in the road, and I suspect most of us at some point ponder those roads not taken. What would our "glimpse" or alternate time line look like had we made different choices in our past? It is true that our lives touch countless others; so what would life look like for them and everyone else affected by the ripple of our actions had we never been born to set things in motion? What would the "holes" look like?

The struggles and battles you've endured in life are important. They've changed you, ultimately for your good and God's glory. They've uniquely equipped you for ministry and calling. I was once advised by a trusted teacher to "give from my void." Essentially, she was telling me that my lack—perceived or real—could be used in the life of another, that there was purpose in my pain. The same can be said for you.

I wonder how different my life would have played out had I never wavered in my faith. Why did I have to be so obstinate and rely on myself for so many years? God didn't have to send ten plagues to bend my knee; He just gave me over to myself, to see what I could accomplish on my own.

And here's what I've learned, a lifeline for you, the thing you need to know and believe in your heart of hearts—even if it doesn't feel like it: God isn't just present in our wilderness, He is praying *for* us, and working *in* us. His Word tells us so.

Therefore, he is able to save completely those who come to God through him, since *he always lives to intercede for them.* (Heb. 7:25, emphasis added)

Who is the one who condemns? Christ Jesus is the one who died, but even more, has been raised; *he also is at the right hand of God and intercedes for us.* (Rom. 8:34, emphasis added)

"I pray not only for these, but also for those who believe in me through their word." (John 17:20, emphasis added)

And these verses give me particular assurance of God's love and concern for me when I'm struggling in my faith:

"Simon, Simon, look out. Satan has asked to sift you like wheat. *But I have prayed for you that your faith may not fail. And you, when you have turned back,* strengthen your brothers." (Luke 22:31–32, emphasis added)

"Lord, *bring us back to yourself, so we may return;* renew our days as in former times." (Lam. 5:21)

There's a presumption of our returning to God, a hint of foregone conclusion, and the hope of us still having something of value to offer others when we do. Yes, there are consequences when we've taken our eyes off Jesus and allowed our lives to revolve around ourselves; but in Christ, those consequences can be for our good, God's glory, and the advance of the gospel. I say this often because I can't hear it enough.

It's tempting to look at a spiritual desert in a negative light, as if it's time wasted. While I wouldn't want to relive my darkest of days, I'm thankful for the holy, refining work that was being accomplished in my life during that season. If given a choice, I wouldn't trade those days because they press the truth of Romans 8:28 into my marrow: "We know that all things work together for the good of those who love God, who are called according to his purpose."

God knew what it would take to get to me, and He knew how my experience could encourage others and bring glory to Him.

God knows what it will take to get *you*. He already knows how your experience will encourage others and glorify Him.

> Blessed be the God and Father of our Lord Jesus Christ, the Father of mercies and the God of all comfort. He comforts us in all our affliction, so that we may be able to comfort those who are in any kind of affliction, through the comfort we ourselves receive from God. For just as the sufferings of Christ overflow to us, so also through Christ our comfort overflows. (2 Cor. 1:3–5)

What a beautiful redemption of hardship or pain.

My heart is more tender toward others because of my undoing. When I wandered far enough away in my faith, reaching the absolute end of myself and all I had to offer in my own strength, when I tumbled off my high and lofty precipice, landsliding into a pit, I met a God who helped me up, squeezed me close, and said, "*Now*, you're where you need to be to know Me as I've always been."

I'm convinced that God allowed me to linger in the desert for so long because He knew I had so much to learn about myself, first, but about Him, most. It wasn't a lesson to be learned quickly and then forgotten almost as fast. Personal losses and relational voids assured I wouldn't become dependent on anything or anyone else but God. During my wander years, I came to understand how it feels to be marginalized, forgotten, rejected, and betrayed. There are many, many more hard things I haven't had to endure that maybe you have or maybe are right now, but I'm convinced those things you think will break you are building faith-muscle. They're transforming you from who you were to who you will be. They're softening and sharpening you in ways a "good" or easy life never could.

Throughout my time as a writer for (in)courage, I've picked up on how often we talk about the idea of "going first." I love this because when we're willing to tell our respective stories, others find the freedom, strength, and courage to tell their own. Strides are made toward hope and healing. As we point one another to Jesus, we celebrate His faithfulness. We see Him working in ways we might otherwise have missed.

> I'm convinced those hard things you think will break you are building faith-muscle. They're transforming you from who you were to who you will be.

Writing this book is me "going first." Honestly, as we near the end of her pages, I'm nervous about some of the things I've shared with you. It's embarrassing to admit my struggle with unbelief, my ugly self-reliance and critical spirit, my pursuit of blogging to make much of myself. I've confided to those close to me that at times revisiting the desert has brought me to tears or made me sick to my stomach. And yet, I'm certain God called me to this work. I'm confident in Him for its timing, the way the opportunity was presented, and all the countless ways He's continued to affirm, encourage, and inspire me page by page, sentence by sentence.

Don't underestimate what God has planned for your future. You can't change your past, but you have today, and, Lord willing, a series of tomorrows. What you've done is behind you; what you can do lies ahead. Jesus Himself is praying for you, eager for you to find Him again (or maybe even for the first time). He will remain faithful to you in your own story, like He remained in mine.

Yours is a wonderful life, my friend, and we need you to do what only you can do. There's not some alternative reality that God placed you in; what you have is what you've got, and God is leading you through your particular struggles and frustrations for a divine purpose. If your life was on the big screen and you could see what a different set of circumstances might produce had you made different choices, you'd see that God knew exactly what He was doing—that what *is* is better than what might have been.

When we point one another to Jesus, we celebrate His faithfulness.

24

ALWAYS REMEMBER

*How many things have to happen to you
before something occurs to you?*[39]
—Robert Frost

Of this I am rather certain: if I had gotten what I thought I
wanted during my wind-chasing years, I would've become an
even worse monster than the one I met overseas, the ugliest version of
myself. God, in His sovereignty, either orchestrating circumstances, or
withholding my dreams, or not allowing them to happen, or however
you want to characterize it, was actually a gift to me. He let me languish
in my own strength and come to the absolute end of myself, stripping
away all the things I was grasping for until all that remained was Him
or nothing.

As I've explained before, when I flirted with choosing "nothing" He
said, "Uhn-uhn, darling girl, you're Mine" and He grabbed hold of me.
Now, if you're in this place of not knowing or believing that He is also
choosing you, if you're doubting all the things of which you used to be
so sure, if your faith is one big knotty tangle, let me encourage you with
a few ancient thoughts:

> "Remember what happened long ago, for I am God, and
> there is no other; I am God, and no one is like me. I declare
> the end from the beginning, and from long ago what is not

yet done, saying: my plan will take place, and I will do all my will." (Isa. 46:9–10)

You don't stand a chance, dear one, when God already has a plan for your doubt, and ultimately, for your life. As John, my former pastor says, "Doubt is not sin, it's simply the lack of evidence at the moment." So right now, as these words flow from my heart through my fingers onto this page, I am standing in the gap for you, praying for evidence to show up and shore up your faith. I know this season feels awful and like it will never end, but it will, and when you get to the other side, you'll look back and finally see that what I'm telling you is true: God was with you and working in you in your wilderness.

> You don't stand a chance, dear one, when God already has a plan for your doubt, and ultimately, for your life.

And while I'm praying for you, I'm going to remind you of some things, because wanderers are a lot like Winnie-the-Pooh when he declared, "I did know once, only I've sort of forgotten."

> God's faithfulness is not dependent on your faith.

First and foremost, God's faithfulness is not dependent on your faith.

If we are faithless, he remains faithful, for he cannot deny himself. (2 Tim. 2:13)

Lord, your faithful love reaches to heaven, your faithfulness to the clouds. (Ps. 36:5)

But you, Lord, are a compassionate and gracious God, slow to anger and abounding in faithful love and truth. (Ps. 86:15)

For the Lord is good, and his faithful love endures forever; his faithfulness, through all generations. (Ps. 100:5)

Your kingdom is an everlasting kingdom; your rule is for all generations. The Lord is faithful in all his words and gracious in all his actions. (Ps. 145:13)

God is faithful; you were called by him into fellowship with his Son, Jesus Christ our Lord. (1 Cor. 1:9)

But the Lord is faithful; he will strengthen and guard you from the evil one. (2 Thess. 3:3)

Let us hold on to the confession of our hope without wavering, since he who promised is faithful. (Heb. 10:23)

So what advantage does the Jew have? Or what is the benefit of circumcision? Considerable in every way. First, they were entrusted with the very words of God. What then? If some were unfaithful, will their unfaithfulness nullify God's faithfulness? Absolutely not! (Rom. 3:1–4a)

Though I've shared a lot of Scripture about God's faithfulness, it is by no means exhaustive.

The second reminder I have for you is to remember Whose you are, and in light of this reality, who you are. Your identity is not defined by your job, your role in your family, or by who others say you are. Your identity isn't about your addictions or habits or propensity to sin; those are things you do.

I was listening to Bryan Stevenson, Founder and Executive Director of the Equal Justice Initiative, speaking to the American College of Trial Lawyers when he struck a nerve about identity. Though he was speaking in the context of justice, I believe the principal also applies to our faith: "Each of us is more than the worst thing we've ever done. I think if someone tells a lie, they're not just a liar. I think even if someone kills someone, they are not just a killer."[40] We will struggle with sin; we will stumble at times and be disobedient.

> Remember Whose you are, and in light of this reality, who you are.

But stumbling doesn't invalidate our salvation; it reminds us of our great need of a Savior, which, in turn, leads us to return to Him. This is repentance.

> Stumbling doesn't invalidate our salvation; it reminds us of our great need of a Savior.

Wandering will finally cease when we fully understand our identity in light of Christ. As a believer, we:

- Bear resemblance to God (Gen. 1:27)
- Are a child of God (John 1:12)
- Are a friend of Jesus (John 15:15)
- Are justified and redeemed (Rom. 3:24)
- God's workmanship (Eph. 2:10. My favorite version is the NLT which calls us God's masterpiece.)
- Are chosen, holy, and blameless in love before God (Eph. 1:4)
- Are adopted as a son through Jesus Christ for Himself (Eph. 1:5)

- Are lavished with grace (Eph. 1:6)
- Are redeemed and forgiven (Eph. 1:7)
- Have received an inheritance (Eph. 1:11)
- Were sealed with the Holy Spirit (Eph. 1:13)
- Were crucified with Christ and no longer enslaved to sin (Rom. 6:6)
- Not condemned (Rom. 8:1)
- Are free from the law of sin and death (Rom. 8:2)
- An heir with Christ (Rom. 8:17)
- Are accepted by Christ (Rom. 15:7)
- Are a temple for the Holy Spirit (1 Cor. 6:19)
- Are one with the Lord (1 Cor. 6:17)
- Are a new creation (2 Cor. 5:17)
- Are the righteousness of God in Christ (2 Cor. 5:21)
- Are free from the bondage of slavery (Gal. 5:1)
- Have citizenship in heaven (Phil. 3:20)

Again, these aren't every passage that reveal our identity in Christ, but they begin to give us the eyes to see ourselves as God sees us, as His beloved children.

The truth about our identity bears repeating because humans are so prone to forget. Then, again, one of Satan's sharpest tools is inflicting memory loss. Or, maybe our ears become calloused from the familiarity of Scripture and we aren't hearing clearly. Maybe we should revisit the counsel of Deuteronomy 6:4–9:

> One of Satan's sharpest tools is inflicting memory loss.

"Listen, Israel: The Lord our God, the Lord is one. Love the Lord your God with all your heart, with all your soul, and with all your strength. These words that I am giving you today are to be in your heart. Repeat them to your children. Talk about them when you sit in your house and when you walk along the road, when you lie down and when you get up. Bind them as a sign on your hand and let them be a symbol on your forehead. Write them on the doorposts of your house and on your city gates."

I urge you to do just that—write down what's true about God and true about you anywhere you can to be a visible reminder that God is faithful even when you're not, that God is who He says He is, and that your identity is different because of Jesus. It is hard to forget Truth when it's everywhere we turn.

25

NOT ALL WHO WANDER
ARE LOST

You yourself have recorded my wanderings.
Put my tears in your bottle. Are they not in your book?
. . . This I know: God is for me.
—Psalm 56:8–9b

I cannot read Psalm 56:8 without adding some more blasted tears to that bottle. Who am I that God is mindful of me? How did we ever find ourselves in a relationship with a "No-matter-what" kind of God? Because of Jesus' finished work on the cross, our faith is secure. It has never been about what I can do but about what Christ has already done, is doing, and will do on my behalf. And for a writer to know that God has recorded her wanderings in a book? I can barely stand it.

I have spent a long, long time wandering, in life and in my faith. I've been battered and bruised by circumstances and people, by both real and perceived loss, and for a little while (or a long while) I let all those things be the boss of me. There is an enemy who delights in our misery, because when we're paying attention to the things that hurt us, we aren't paying attention to God. We might as well be staring at the rain in our backyard when there's a beautiful, baby rainbow in the front. And that, my friends, is when we go off the rails. We end up playing a victim instead of the victors we are.

I don't know if God caused or allowed my years in the desert, but it doesn't really matter. They accomplished hard and holy work, a refining by fire, fueling a faith that barely existed in that season. Having the freedom to doubt and wrestle and ask questions strengthened my faith and it's brought me to a new level of trust in God. My experience helps me to shout "Yes!" when James challenges believers to, "Consider it a great joy, my brothers and sisters, whenever you experience various trials, because you know that the testing of your faith produces endurance. And let endurance have its full effect, so that you may be mature and complete, lacking nothing" (James 1:2–4).

Maybe it's the comparison game all over again that sends us stumbling into a spiritual desert, with us judging our faith as too small to be "real." But Jesus has something to say about that; when it comes to faith, pretty small is just enough. In fact, in the Gospels of Matthew, Mark, and Luke, He repeatedly suggests that tiny faith the size of a mustard seed isn't simply just enough to get by, but instead, can accomplish great things. Consider how these tiniest of seeds produce the largest of trees so birds can nest and make their home in its branches. Or, command a mountain to move from here to there. Or, uproot a mulberry tree and replant it in the sea just by speaking to it.

Even small faith can be explosive.

I think this is Jesus' way of saying dynamite comes in small packages. Even small faith can be explosive.

At forty, we had moved to a new place and started all over again in a place where we knew no one. As fate would have it, the same thing happened the year we turned fifty. I know seven is considered a year of completion in Scripture, but to me there's something complete about a decade, and not just any block of ten years, but milestone birthdays. My season of wandering took place in my forties, and I am finding a season of abundance in my fifties.

It is a precious grace to me that God brought healing to me through community, the very thing that I longed for but had eluded me for so long. I can only explain what happened as a Joel 2:25 sort of thing, "Then I will make up to you for the years that the swarming locust has eaten . . ." (NASB). He gave me the last thing I ever expected to receive in this new place: a pile of iron—a group of women who consistently challenge and encourage me in my faith, pray for me often, and love me enough to tell me things I need to hear . . . even when I don't want to. They are a gift, and when I've spent time with them, I want more of Jesus. Our initial meetings seemed so random, but God knew my heart and my needs, and He has more than made up the years those wretched locusts devoured. I'm also stewarding my relationships differently these days, careful not to take them for granted and mindful they don't take the place reserved for God alone. He is my greatest gift.

If you are in the lonely place right now, I am praying for you, both as I pen these words and in the days to come. I'm intimately acquainted with those complicated feelings of seeing others who seem to have it all when you don't, whether the "all" is a successful career, a flawless marriage, perfect children, or a close-knit community. Be careful . . . what you perceive may not be reality, and it's definitely not the entire picture.

No matter what else you do, seek first the kingdom of God and His righteousness (Matt. 6:33). It is evidence of growth, transformation, wisdom, and maturity when you (finally) pursue the Giver and not the gifts. God could provide for you in the same way and timing He has for me, but even more likely, your story will look different than mine. Regardless, I can promise you this: God is working in your wandering.

> It is evidence of growth, transformation, wisdom, and maturity when you pursue the Giver and not the gifts.

He will restore your soul in the end, however He sees fit and in His perfect way.

Satan loves it when we have questions or doubts about God, and his hope is that we'll never find our way back. I'm more than happy to inform him that my wandering is the very thing God used to draw me closer. That Satan would even care to mess with me tells me God has something magnificent in store for my life. I'm convinced He has the same for you. If you find yourself in the desert, just wait for how He'll use your story. It is in my story and yours that I see the truth and significance of Romans 8:28–32:

> We know that all things work together for the good of those who love God, who are called according to his purpose. For those he foreknew he also predestined to be conformed to the image of his Son, so that he would be the firstborn among many brothers and sisters. And those he predestined, he also called; and those he called, he also justified; and those he justified, he also glorified. What then are we to say about these things? If God is for us, who is against us? He did not even spare his own Son but offered him up for us all. How will he not also with him grant us everything?

God is for us in our wandering; He's working all things together for good.

It's important to fess up and tell you I still struggle with unbelief. I'm afraid I'm one of those who might always find a tension in my faith, but I've learned that isn't necessarily a bad thing. My doubts ultimately led me back to God, and they continue to do so. It's becoming clearer and

> God is for us in our wandering; He's working all things together for good.

clearer to me that seeking God in response to the tension between belief and unbelief is an indication of maturity, not a sign of weakness.

You might have already noticed that the title of this book comes from a poem in J. R. R. Tolkien's *The Lord of the Rings*. Certainly, if you've read the books, you'll understand its contextual significance, but even if not, I think you'll appreciate it:

> All that is gold does not glitter,
> Not all those who wander are lost;
> The old that is strong does not wither,
> Deep roots are not reached by the frost.
> From the ashes, a fire shall be woken,
> A light from the shadows shall spring;
> Renewed shall be blade that was broken,
> The crownless again shall be king.[41]

Even if you're in a season of wandering or on the see-saw of belief/unbelief, where you are today is bringing you one step closer to where you'll always be. Remember, Christ Himself is praying for your return to Him, and He will reveal more of Himself when you seek and ask.

God is for you, dear one, and His love makes you more than a conqueror in this season of struggle. More than that, He promises that not even the wander years can separate you from His love (Rom. 8:37–39).

If you're wandering in a spiritual desert, I'm convinced The Way *is* the way out. Why am I so sure? Let's consider a few things we've learned in my story, perhaps what your head already knows that your heart is slowly figuring out:

One, God is faithful even when you aren't. He will show up when you might have missed Him, when you need Him, when you seek Him. He is going to reach out and grab hold of you if you slip to the end of your rope and even think about letting go. It's who He is.

If you're wandering in a spiritual desert, The Way *is* the way out.

And two, knowing God is the key to life. Not knowing *about* Him. Not being able to spout off Scripture or recite the Apostles' Creed or knowing all the right Christian things to say or do. But personally knowing Him and being transformed as a result, and understanding that His faithfulness isn't a function of your faith. Coming to know God truly and deeply is well worth whatever cost it took to deepen your relationship.

The well-known words of John Piper tell us, "God is most glorified in you when you are most satisfied in Him." [41] How can we be satisfied in someone we don't intimately know? My praise and prayer for all of us is inspired and guided by Philippians 3:8–10a (my emphasis added):

> I also consider everything to be a loss in view of the surpassing value of knowing Christ Jesus my Lord. Because of him I have suffered the loss of all things and consider them as dung, so that I may gain Christ and be found in him, not having a righteousness of my own from the law, but one that is through faith in Christ—the righteousness from God based on faith. *My goal is to know him . . .*

Oh, that we could say that and mean it.

Maybe your conversion testimony, like mine, isn't as spectacular as Paul's Damascus Road, but maybe your season of struggle is the story your coworker, fellow church-goer, neighbor, or family needs to hear. God is always, *always* glorified when our stories—even those characterized by wrestling and wander—display His greatness and faithfulness. (I hope to hear yours one day.)

And, maybe, just maybe, you're coming to realize that, indeed, you're a lot like I was—a wanderer, a temporary desert dweller, a scraggly little ragamuffin, a questioner, or a doubter. Proclaim it with me: *"Lord, I believe. Help my unbelief."*

Thankfully, He not only hears that heartfelt prayer, He answers it. A wanderer is always on the move somewhere, and God will lead the honest seeker right back to Himself. Once you emerge on the other side, you'll find that you were given a gift—the chance to really know the God who is faithful to the wanderer.

NOTES

1. Lyrics by Richard Rodgers and Oscar Hammerstein, sung by Julie Andrews, "Do-Re-Mi." *The Sound of Music*, 45th Anniverary Edition (Sony Legacy, 2010). Audio CD.

2. This translation of Dante's *The Divine Comedy: The Inferno, Purgatorio, and Paradiso* comes from the Everyman's Library Series, translated by Allen Mandelbaum and introduced by Peter Armour (New York: Knopf Doubleday Publishing Group, 1995).

3. This phrase was taken from the script of *The Greatest Showman*, on page 36, provided by Jenny Bicks at Scripts.com: https://www.scripts.com /script-pdf/20368.

4. Jocelyn Voo, "How Birth Order Affects Your Child's Personality and Behavior," *Parents Magazine*, https://www.parents.com/baby/development/ social/birth-order-and-personality/.

5. "Amazing Grace," words and music by John Newton (1779), public domain.

6. Olayinka Dada, *Blossom: Abounding in God's Master Plan of Fruitfulness* (Chester, NY: Dunamis, 2012).

7. C. S. Lewis, *The Four Loves* (New York: Harcourt Brace and Company, 1960), 65.

8. Benjamin Franklin, *Poor Richard's Almanack* (Waterloo, IA: The U.S.C. Publishing Company, 1914), 16.

9. https://www.barna.com/research/half-churchgoers-not-heard-great -commission/?utm_source=Barna+Update+List&utm_campaign=3838fdc080 -WELCOME__1&utm_medium=email&utm_term=0_8560a0e52e -3838fdc080-180719081&mc_cid=3838fdc080&mc_eid=e830884c96

10. This line comes from George Harrison's song "Any Road," *Brainwashed* (Parlophone, Dark Horse, 2003).

11. Dr. Tony Evans posted this on his own Instagram page at https:// www.instagram.com/p/BlsqhNPgEid/.

12. Commonly attributed to C. S. Lewis in *Prince Caspian*, but disputed without further attribution.

13. T. S. Eliot in his poem "Burnt Norton," within the greater work *Four Quartets* (New York: Houghton Mifflin Harcourt, 1943), 13.

14. Charles R. Swindoll, *Improving Your Serve: The Art of Unselfish Living* (Nashville, TN: W Publishing Group, 1981).

15. There's debate over whether Angelou actually said this first. It has also been attributed to Carl William Buehner too.

16. Jean Fleming, *Pursue the Intentional Life* (Colorado Springs, CO: NavPress, 2013), 16.

17. Ibid.

18. Jean de La Fontaine, *Fables*, ebook release date 1/7/18, Book VIII Fable VI, 377. Fontaine actually wrote this volume in 1678/79.

19. Lewis, *The Four Loves*, 65.

20. J. B. Priestly, *The Reader's Digest*, Volume 118, Issue 1, 175.

21. This quotation comes from an interview published on Barnabas Piper's website. The interview between Barnabas Piper and Justin Holcomb: https://barnabaspiper.com/2015/06/the-best-quotes-on-belief-and-doubt.html.

22. The earliest version of this well-known phrase was found on a Christian tract used in Germany in AD 1627, authored by Rupertus Meldenius to promote unity during the divisive and chaotic period of the Thirty Years War, http://faculty.georgetown.edu/jod/augustine/quote.html.

23. Gary Chapman, "The Five Love Languages Defined," Blogpost, June 6, 2018, https://www.5lovelanguages.com/2018/06/the-five-love-languages-defined/.

24. https://www.compassion.com/about/what-is-compassion.htm

25. https://www.compassion.com/about/in-jesus-name.htm

26. Spurgeon's sermons, Volume 38, 1892. This content has been made public at https://www.ccel.org/ccel/spurgeon/sermons38.xlvi.html.

27. Gary Chapman, *The Five Love Languages* (Chicago, IL: Northfield Publishing, 1992).

28. Gary Chapman, "The Five Love Languages Defined," Blogpost, June 6, 2018, https://www.5lovelanguages.com/2018/06/the-five-love-languages-defined/.

29. Corrie Ten Boom is known to have recited this often-used phrase from her sister Betsie. See https://christianhistoryinstitute.org/magazine /article/there-is-no-pit-so-deep.

30. John Eldredge, *Waking the Dead: The Glory a Heart Fully Alive* (Nashville, TN: Thomas Nelson, 2016).

31. Kings Kaleidoscope, "Rain" on *The Beauty Between* (Independent, 2017).

32. https://www.telegraph.co.uk/culture/film/8223925/127-Hours -Aron-Ralstons-story-of-survival.html

33. John Calvin, *Institutes of the Christian Religion*, Book III, Ch 2.15, from Christian Classics Ethereal Library (Grand Rapids, MI: public domain), http://www.ccel.org/ccel/calvin/institutes.html.

34. Barnabas Piper, *Help My Unbelief: Why Doubt Is Not the Enemy of Faith* (Colorado Springs, CO: David C Cook, 2015), 27–28.

35. C. S. Lewis, *God in the Dock: Essays on Theology and Ethics* (Grand Rapids, MI/Cambridge, UK: William B. Eerdman's Publishing Co., 2014), 13. Original book was published in 1970.

36. Some books attribute this to an ancient African proverb, while others attribute it to an ancient Chinese proverb. Various articles online also use it this way, though the original source is unknown.

37. *It's a Wonderful Life*, directed by Frank Capra (Liberty Films, 1946).

38. Rob Greitens, "Are You a Miracle? On the Probability of You Being Born, posted 6/16/11, https://www.academia.edu/4982879/Are_You_a_Miracle_ On_the_Probability_of_Your_Being_Born_Posted_06_16_11_04_55_ PM_ET_Read_more.

39. Robert Frost's friend, Edward Hyde Cox, quoted this phrase from Frost: https://www.nytimes.com/1976/08/30/archives/robert-frost-gets-his -road-and-his-day-in-vermont.html.

40. Bryan Stevenson, Founder and Executive Director of the Equal Justice Initiative, Speaking to the American College of Trial Lawyers for their 2017 Spring Meeting, YouTube, https://www.youtube.com/watch ?v=FINmQ0lmXGM.

41. J. R. R. Tolkien, *The Lord of the Rings: Part One, The Fellowship of the Ring* (UK: Allen &Unwin, 1954, 1965, 1966), 193.

42. John Piper, *Desiring God* (Colorado Springs, CO: Multnomah, 2011), 10.

LET'S CONNECT!

A former marketing and PR professional, Robin Dance now encourages others in life and faith as a writer, speaker, and small group leader. She believes listening well, laughter, and generosity are indispensable super-powers, and there might not be a sweeter ministry than a gift of home-baked bread. Robin advocated for children in poverty as a Compassion International blogger in Kolkata, and she has been a regular contributor to (in)courage, DaySpring's online community for women, since its inception. Married to her college sweetheart and mom to a daughter and two sons, Robin is a fan of good stories, and her favorite is the one you're dying to share.

robindance.me

robindance.me

facebook.com/RobinBDance

robindance

Robin@robindance.me

#ForAllWhoWanderBook

Use the Journey Guide
to help you, your book club,
or your small group navigate
your own faith journey,
discovering how much
For All Who Wander
is specifically for you.

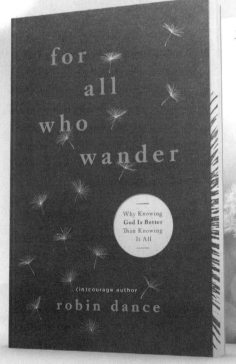

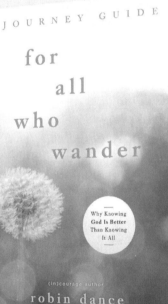

(in)courage welcomes you

to a place where authentic, brave women connect deeply with God and others. Through the power of shared stories and meaningful resources, (in)courage champions women and celebrates the strength Jesus gives to live out our calling as God's daughters. In the middle of your unfine moments and ordinary days, you are invited to become a woman of courage.

Join us at **www.incourage.me** and connect with us on social media!

f 🐦 📷 📌
@incourage

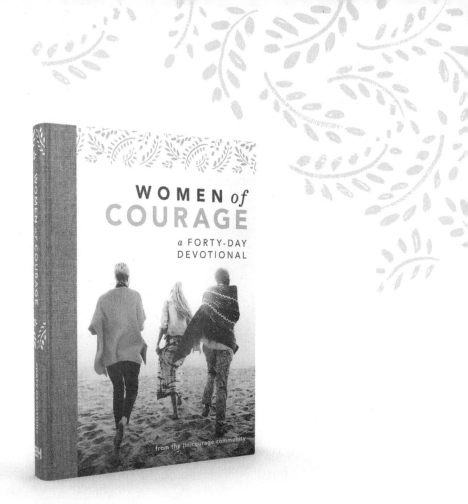

You are a Woman *of* Courage...
Because God says so.

Featuring 40 brave women from the Bible, this devotional will walk with you through the hardest days and leave you with the courage you need to lead, to love, to trust, and to turn to God in every situation.

Available now wherever books are sold.